ANTHONY JOSHUA

FRANK WORRALL is Britain's No. 1 sports biographer and writes exclusively for John Blake Publishing. He is the author of nineteen books on sport, including the bestselling *Jamie Vardy: The Boy From Nowhere*, *Roy Keane: Red Man Walking*, *Rooney: Wayne's World*, *Celtic United: Glasgow and Manchester*, *Lewis Hamilton: Triple World Champion – The Biography* and *Rory McIlroy – The Biography*. Rock star Rod Stewart once hailed *Celtic United* as 'the last good book I read'. Frank's website frankworrall.com has details of all his books and he can be found at @frankworrall on Twitter.

FROM THE STREETS TO HEAVYWEIGHT CHAMPION

ANTHONY JOSHUA
KING OF THE RING

FRANK WORRALL

JOHN BLAKE

Published by John Blake Publishing,
3 Bramber Court, 2 Bramber Road,
London W14 9PB, England

www.johnblakebooks.com

www.facebook.com/johnblakebooks
twitter.com/jblakebooks

First published in paperback in 2017

ISBN: 978-1-78606-542-1

British Library Cataloguing-in-Publication Data:

A catalogue record for this book is available from the British Library.

Design by www.envydesign.co.uk

Printed in Great Britain by CPI Group (UK) Ltd

1 3 5 7 9 10 8 6 4 2

Papers used by John Blake Publishing are natural, recyclable products made from
wood grown in sustainable forests. The manufacturing processes conform to the
environmental regulations of the country of origin.

Every attempt has been made to contact the relevant copyright-holders,
but some were unobtainable. We would be grateful if the appropriate people
could contact us.

John Blake Publishing is an imprint of Bonnier Publishing
www.bonnierpublishing.com

This book is dedicated to Toby Buchan,
a brilliant editor and a true gent.

CONTENTS

ACKNOWLEDGEMENTS

Many thanks: all at John Blake Publishing, Jon Moorhead, Ross 'Biscuit' Harris, Dave Kidd, Pat Sheehan, Danny Bottono, Dominic Turnbull, Dave Morgan, John Maskey, Wes Smith, Tony Grassby, Jo Porter, Graham Oates, Andy Clayton, Steven Gordon, Ian Rondeau, Ben Felsenburg, Alex Butler, Lee Clayton, Roy Stone, Colin Forshaw, Tom Henderson Smith, Lee Hassall.

Heartfelt thanks: Angela, Frankie, Jude and Natalie, Frank and Barbara, Bob and Stephen.

CHAPTER 1

THE BEGINNING

'You cannot not love this man. He's turned his life around,
won Olympic gold, he lives with his mum in north London . . .
he's already got plenty of money, he just wants to stay
there and dedicate his life to the sport.'
— ANTHONY JOSHUA'S PROMOTER, EDDIE HEARN .

29 April 2017

There's a sequence in the movie *Rocky IV* where Apollo Creed enters the arena wearing an Uncle Sam outfit, replete with outrageous top hat, dancing and shadow boxing to the James Brown classic, 'Living In America'. Creed, now 42, has been trained by Rocky for an exhibition bout against the Russian Ivan Drago and is determined to give the fans something to remember. He smiles and laughs and salutes his fans. Only Drago hasn't come for an exhibition match; he has come trained for destruction and for a literal fight to the death with Creed.

It is one of the most stunning entrances to a fight ever and the following sequence, in which Drago does not even blink when Creed winks to him as if to say, 'We're here to play, this isn't a real fight,' makes the film-goer hold his or her breath in anticipation of a potential tragedy. Two men, one in the ring for fun, the other for deadly business. It soon becomes clear that Drago is emotionless and that Creed has made a terrible miscalculation. He should have taken the fight seriously, but allowed himself to get carried by the notion that he is here for nothing more than a visual and musical display to please the crowd, and that Drago is in on the secret. There then follows the crushing realisation when Drago thumps him into oblivion, and utters the prophetic, sinister phrase, 'If he dies, he dies.'

Fast forward to Saturday, 29 April 2017. London heavyweight champion Anthony Joshua, holder of the IBF belt and Olympic champion, enters the capital's Wembley Stadium in front of 90,000-plus adoring fans. He saunters down towards the ring in a flashy satin white robe with music from rapper Stormzy as his backing track. But instead of jumping straight in the ring he detours onto a platform that raises him up into the warm night air, with Jack White's 'Seven Nation Army' now his accompaniment. Then comes the denouement, as flames explode and Anthony salutes the crowd, with his initials AJ on either side in full pyrotechnic glory. Meanwhile, the modern-day 'Beast from the East' stands proudly in the ring, awaiting his arrival, face stern and emotionless, ready to do battle like a real-life Drago.

The similarities with the scene from *Rocky IV* made many of Fleet Street's finest a tad nervous for Anthony's health and safety. Had he blown it before he even unleashed an initial punch? Sure, the crowd loved the spectacle and Anthony, commonly known as 'AJ', revelled in the adulation. But wouldn't it have hit him emotionally, blurring his focus? And wouldn't it have wound up the emotionless, totally focused and determined Ukrainian in the opposite corner? Wladimir Klitschko was no journeyman. He was by far the toughest, most decorated opponent AJ had faced. Not for nothing was he known as 'Dr Steelhammer', and not for nothing did he hold the record of having the second longest reign in boxing history.

Klitschko, also an Olympic champion, had trained harder than any time in his career for this fight, determined as he was to regain his world crown and, more importantly for such a noble man, his pride after his shock loss to Britain's Tyson Fury. In the eyes of many pundits, and his corner, he was in the best shape of his career and his threat to AJ was a very real one. Wladimir was, and is, a boxer who, unlike the vast majority, had interests outside the fight game and who liked to view his fights tactically and technically, not just in terms of sheer brawn. So it was little wonder that he simply smiled and shook his head knowingly as AJ walked the final yards to the ring, after his showbiz arrival. Klitschko had seen it all in his years at the top; he might be 41 but he looked ten years younger as he and AJ touched gloves.

This was the final leg of a journey for Anthony Joshua – a journey that had begun in a 'spit and sawdust' gym in Finchley, North London, in 2008 and would end, hopefully in triumph, against one of the greatest world champions of any era in England's national stadium. Could AJ deliver, or had he blown it with that flashy, Apollo Creed-style entrance? Had he the guts, talent and determination to switch on to the fight, or had the pyrotechnics, glamour and sheer adulation dulled the aggression within? Even if he has lost focus temporarily, it could be fatal against a predator like Klitschko. Or had the over-the-top show actually filled him with more pride and more determination to show his gratitude to those loyal fans who had splashed out big money to see him in action on the biggest night of his life?

We were about to find out. But one thing was for sure . . . Anthony Joshua had turned his life around and found redemption against the odds. He had swapped a life of petty criminality and potential jail terms to become a figure much loved by the British public for his immensely likeable personality, and by boxing fans as Britain's greatest ever fighter. He had the likeability of Frank Bruno out of the ring and the swaggering, no-fear, witty potential of a British Muhammad Ali inside it. But just how had he got there – how had he come to sell 90,000 tickets for a boxing bout in London to come up against a great champion? How had he done all this from humble beginnings and a total lack of direction that almost led to him ending up in prison? From Watford to Wembley via Nigeria, Finchley and Reading jail, this is one of the greatest rags-to-riches, and to ultimate redemption, stories of our times . . .

15 October 1989

It was a normal, dull, wet yet mild October Sunday in Watford, a town roughly 20 miles north-west of London. Some locals headed out for normal, dull, yet mild outings, including trips to the town's DIY stores and food supermarkets or, if time permitted, garden centres. Others preferred the sanctuary of home and the likes of *EastEnders* or the golf from Wentworth on the telly, while still more enjoyed a brisk walk with the dog and a relaxing pint down the local boozer. But for Yeta Odusanya, 15

October 1989, would be a day like no other – for it was the day she gave birth to a boy who, against all odds, would become one of the most famous people in her adopted homeland, respected and loved in equal measure for his gentle personality yet fierce boxing spirit.

Yeta, a social worker who came to Britain from Nigeria in the 1990s, cried tears of joy as she held Anthony Oluwafemi Olaseni Joshua in her arms that day. His father, Robert, who is half-Nigerian, half-Irish, was also thrilled that he had another son. The happy parents had arrived in Watford from Nigeria while in their early 20s and also had another son and two daughters. When Yeta took Anthony home to the council flat where they lived on Watford's tough Meriden estate, she would dance around the living room with him in her arms as the radio blasted out Lisa Stansfield's 'All Around The World' or the Rebel MC's hip-hop classic 'Street Tuff'.

She would show him off to friends who commented that he was a 'lovable, big, chunky baby, who always had a smile for you'. His parents split up, reportedly when he was four or five, and he continued to live with mum Yeta, who witnessed his growth spurts and continual demands for more food! In one famous picture, in his high chair at home, he is seen demolishing two large bowls packed with mashed potatoes and spinach. He was 18 months old, but could have passed for double his age, such was his size.

The boy was strong as well as big and soon graduated from his high chair to running around the flat and then playing outside with other youngsters. Back then, he was known as Femi rather than Anthony, and by the age of five or six loved playing football and having rough-and-tumbles with his cousin, Ben Ileyemi, who would also go on to be a fine boxer; indeed, he would become the man who introduced AJ to the fight game that would transform both their lives. 'He was always active,' Ben would later recall. 'He was always playing football or whatever. We used to scrap and I would get the better of him. Things have changed. We were messing around a couple of years ago and he hit me in the ribs. I never actually told him at the time but I was in pain for about four days. Imagine taking a scaffolding pole and wrapping a pillowcase on the end, then getting wacked with it. That's what it is like. But back then he was just a big lad who wanted to be outside.'

In the year 2000, Anthony's steady life in Watford was shattered when Yeta decided to return to Nigeria. She felt it would benefit her son who, aged 11, had allegedly started drinking and getting into trouble on the estate. He was enrolled in a boarding school in Nigeria, but did not enjoy the stay one bit, leaving after only one term. No wonder, really, for he was forced to fetch water every morning at 5.30 a.m. Sure, there is something to be said for enforcing discipline, but that went way beyond the norm. It was bullying. He would later say of his time at the school, 'Sometimes the whole block would just get punished. It might be the cane, or you would have to squat and hold it for 30 minutes. We got beaten, but that's my culture, beating.'

Yeta now had another decision to make. Anthony had clearly been unhappy with his new life in Nigeria and she opted to return with him to Watford. He was now enrolled in Kings Langley School in the town, and felt much more at home and happy, especially as he quickly excelled in sport. Anthony would hold the Year 9 record of 11.6 seconds in the 100 metres race and even nowadays his record of running the 400m in a minute in Year 8, when he was 12, still stands.

He was also an extremely talented footballer and even went for a trial with Charlton Athletic. Yet any dreams of a career in the beautiful game, where he was excelling as a centre-forward, ended abruptly when he attacked an opponent who had been teasing him. A formal complaint to the police was made, as a result of which Anthony, aged 16, received a warning as to his future conduct. He had grabbed the rival by the neck, hauled him above his shoulder and then let him drop to the ground.

It was a worrying period of Anthony's life, especially for his mum who had such big dreams for her big boy. She knew he had a heart of gold and just needed some direction in his life – if he had a target he was more than capable of going for it with total dedication. But his tendency towards violence, which would stand him in good stead in the boxing ring, was unfortunately earning him a reputation as a lad who was a hothead with an uncontrollable temper. He was mixing in the wrong circles and seemed to be going nowhere – except maybe prison if he did not heed that warning.

Anthony appeared out of control, he did not heed the warning and it did not help that when mum Yeta upped sticks for Golders Green, North London, he decided to stay put in Watford. He was 16 and alone in a town where he had already been in trouble and where he seemed to be drifting towards more difficulties. He stayed with friends and in hostels and his lifestyle was the exact opposite of the clean-living, disciplined approach he would adopt when he became a professional boxer. He smoked, drank, partied and lived on the edge as part of a reckless gang in the town. Anthony hit a new low the following year, when a street fight brought him to another brush with the law and a brief spell in Reading jail. The prison had, in previous times, held the author and wit Oscar Wilde, but AJ's incarceration was nothing to write home about. He was 17 and, by his own account, spent two weeks on remand for 'fighting and other stuff'.

As with the incident a year earlier, fate shone compassionately on him, for he had feared he might end up with a prison sentence. One consequence was that he was fitted with an electronic tag, which he would have to wear for a year. But redemption was rearing its head. In a moment of clarity, he realised living in Watford and being in a gang was not conducive to a better life. He had been banned from Watford town centre, so was limited anyway as to what he could do at night, and where he could go. As with most towns in England, the centre of Watford was where his mates congregated and where the main 'action' was. So he left the town for good and went to live with his mum in Golders Green. It was a new start and it would open a window to a new life – in the boxing world.

His cousin Ben Ileyemi lived in the vicinity and was well aware of the problems his wayward relative had encountered. He himself had prospered through the discipline that joining a local amateur boxing club had brought and he reckoned it would benefit Anthony, too. So he persuaded AJ to go with him to Finchley and District Amateur Boxing Club and Anthony was intrigued and excited by what he found. He then famously borrowed some money from Ben to buy some boxing boots and started to learn the ropes of the sport. Finally, he had found something that he was not only good at, but that also he wanted wholeheartedly to commit to. 'I started reading because I learned that so many champions educated themselves. Joe Louis, Mike Tyson, Bernard Hopkins,' he would tell the *Guardian* in 2015. 'Before it was "act now, think later" – but the discipline and reading changed me.'

Anthony was working hard to change. He had started working as a bricklayer and attended the boxing club every night. He was determined to make it in the fight game but knew he needed an income, so worked whenever he could as a brickie. He was being responsible and trying to turn his life around. The club's trainers, led by the inimitable Sean Murphy, were impressed by how AJ buckled down and that he was so eager to listen and learn. They knew he had the brute strength to progress and that he would be hard to beat. But he was a rough diamond and had to be taught when to throw a punch, and when to defend, when to jab and when to go in for the kill. As a teenager he had got into trouble because he acted without thinking, but now he was learning fast that to survive and thrive as a boxer you needed much more than simple aggression. That would get you so far, but it would not work against boxers who were just as strong but far more streetwise.

That was why he was willing to take in what Sean had to say and why he was studying tapes of the greatest professional champions. His aim was not simply to be a good boxer; he was a perfectionist, so it was important to be the best. As his life changed, so did his self-esteem and character. After a few years off the rails, he once again became the lovable boy who could charm anyone, much to his mother's obvious delight.

Yeta was pleased to see him so committed to his boxing and that he finally had a target to aim for, and that he was happy doing something he loved. Sure, she worried about him getting hurt in the ring, but she knew that he was as strong as an ox and that he could look after himself. Her anxiety would be one of the reasons he never allowed her to watch him fight as he progressed up the ranks. He felt it could affect his own performance if he, in turn, was worried about how his mum was reacting ringside.

Over the years he had become very close to her and she would remain the most important person in his life as he climbed ever higher up the boxing rankings. He trusted her and knew she always had his best interests at heart. He was a mum's boy and would always try to repay her for the efforts she had put into bringing him up alone. He owed her, and when he finally made some money as a pro he would buy her the Golders Green flat. Even when he became world champion, he would go back to living with her in the flat. It was very touching and emphasised just how much loyalty meant to Anthony Joshua. His mum had been the one person who had always stuck by him, through thick and thin, and he would always remember that and be grateful to her.

The boxing was going well, the bricklaying not as well. Anthony had taken on a few bouts and won them convincingly (apart from the infamous one that saw his most bitter rival Dillian Whyte beat him). He was learning how to pace himself and how to defend. He already knew how to punch hard but was told by his trainer not to punch himself out too quickly, as he risked being fatigued within a couple of rounds. That did not stop him regularly going for the quick knockout and would, some critics contend, leave him open to precisely the problem Sean Murphy had warned him about: getting too tired too quickly (in some of his latter-day pro fights, those concerns would become real when his bouts went beyond two rounds, although he would deal with them by coming back strong after drawing breath).

His aim was to make the GB squad and compete in international tournaments. The 2012 Olympics would be in London – and what bigger dream was there than that for a lad like Anthony Joshua? He knew it would be hard work but he was, as always, totally confident in himself and his ability. But first he had to keep on winning at club level: that way he would get himself known to the selectors and become a realistic contender. He did keep winning and the selectors did take note, eventually adding his name to their squad. By 2010 he was making such progress that his name was now being touted as a real possibility for the Olympics.

Then, just as everything was going well and the future was looking bright, Anthony typically shot himself in the foot with another act of self-sabotage. After all the advances in his career and life, he still could not shake off the past completely. In 2011, he was pulled up by police for speeding in his car and they found 8 ounces of cannabis in his bag. He was charged with possession of the drug but wrongly also charged with intent to supply a Class B drug. Anthony received a 12-month community order and was ordered to carry out 100 hours of unpaid work. He pleaded guilty to possession of cannabis and was suspended from boxing.

He was not a household name, or even an easily recognisable sporting figure, but the police had no problem in identifying him

– as he was wearing his GB boxing tracksuit at the time of his arrest. It seriously looked as if he might now walk away from boxing and return to Watford and the gang life. But something pulled him back from the edge – maybe the love he had for his mother, whom he desperately did not want to hurt any further after the way she had continually supported him, and also the respect he had for his coaches up at Finchley. Sean Murphy's fellow trainer at the club, John Oliver, explained how AJ didn't throw it all away in a moment of further madness. He told the *Daily Mail*, 'Sean and I took him aside so many times to tell him to give up whatever he was doing out there. That last one, though, was the real wake-up call. He was doing his community service in North Finchley, on an allotment next to my house. I used to sit with him in my car when he was done and talk about what he was doing with his life. The way he responded to what happened, I couldn't be prouder.'

The penny had finally dropped. This would be the final indiscretion. Anthony realised he was in the last-chance saloon – if he could survive this and get his boxing career on track he vowed to his mother and to his trainers that he would never let them, or himself, down again. He had been lucky to come through his two earlier brushes with the law; now he was hoping and praying for a third chance. If he did not get it, he could possibly have returned to his old ways, but fortune favoured him once again.

Team GB believed in him and decided to give him another chance, even as he was doing his community-order work. He was chosen to take part in the European championships and duly reached the quarter-finals. He admitted that the call-up was a big turning point, telling *The Times*, 'They had banned me from all boxing internationally and domestically for my club. I thought I'm done with boxing. So I went back to Watford and started hanging around with my mates. But that's when GB Boxing called me up and asked if I want to go to the Europeans. They said, "We're still looking into your case . . ." So I had a week's training and then lost in the quarter-finals.

'It was a turning point. Before the world championships I said, "Man, I have to change. I have an opportunity with boxing that I believe in. I am going to focus all my energies in boxing." I was 21 and I'd had my share of problems,' he said, referring to his earlier encounters with the law.

Anthony won silver at the World Championships, a feat that earned him a place in Team GB's boxing squad for the 2012 Olympics. That silver win not only changed AJ's life, it saved it, according to his promoter, Eddie Hearn, 'That was a big turning point for him,' Eddie would tell the *Daily Telegraph*. 'Look, he's a bad guy trying to be good. And he needs to be a bad boy, and retain that to get to where he wants to be in the ring. But boxing has saved his life. He's a pure example of it. It's given him discipline, a focus for that huge physique and desire to fight.'

Now there would be no turning back to the lifestyle that had left Anthony on the brink of criminality. He was heading to the very top and would even be predicted to become boxing's first billionaire. But first he had to negotiate the amateurs, and then hopefully star for his country at the London Olympics. He was finally on the right track, but a hell of a lot of work lay ahead if he was to fulfil his remarkable potential, and even one day justify entering Wembley Apollo Creed-style for a date with boxing's real-life Ivan Drago . . .

CHAPTER 2

SAVED BY THE BELL

'If it weren't for boxing, I would have been
in drug gangs and prison,'
– ANTHONY JOSHUA

Boxing would truly prove to be the saviour of Anthony Joshua, getting him off the streets and out of trouble with the cops. It would provide him with a solid route to redemption, to turn his life around and to transform himself from a person some considered 'a bad'un' into a respected individual with much self-esteem, and whom fellow athletes would eventually look up to and try to emulate. It was a wonderful tale of light from darkness and it helped mould the man we see today – a witty, likeable guy who is also a fine purveyor of boxing skills – and to put him on a pedestal for many fans of boxing, and young boxers themselves.

The journey towards the light would begin in 2007 when AJ's cousin encouraged him to take up the sport. Anthony was working as a jobbing bricklayer when Ben Ileyemi suggested he might want to take a look at the boxing club where he hung out.

Ben had noticed that Anthony seemed restless and that his life wasn't going in a direction he would have hoped. He also saw that Anthony, then 17, could have the attributes to make it as a fighter. He was tough, not fearful and a fine athlete. At school, Anthony had been good at football and had even run 100 metres in a more than commendable 11.6 seconds.

His instinctive sporting talent, size and growing physique said to his cousin that this was a boy who could find a new direction if he could catch the boxing bug. So Ben persuaded AJ to accompany him to Finchley and District Amateur Boxing Club and to see exactly what boxing was all about. It would prove to be a turning point in both men's lives. It was the start of Anthony's journey from teenage tearaway to respected world champion and Ben would also benefit, ending up working with his cousin as he moved ever upwards. And if anyone deserved a break with AJ, it was surely Ben, who had helped him escape from a life on the edge.

Ben had coaxed him in with the prospect of improving his fitness – via a fitness class and lifting weights. It was an inspired move as it put Anthony in the midst of a boxing world Ben was convinced would appeal to his giant of a cousin. The club is renowned for producing top boxers and for its top trainers. It advertises itself like this on a promotional site, 'The gym has consistently been producing schoolboy, national and international amateur champions up to Olympic level. It has also trained and produced world rated professional boxers of the calibre of Spencer "The Omen" Oliver (who is now regularly on the Sky Sports panel offering expert analysis and commentary on all the major fights from around the world).

Also, ex-British champion Sean Murphy – who challenged Steve Robinson for the world featherweight title). Come here to train with fully qualified boxing coaches. Fitness and weight training also provided.'

British heavyweight Dereck Chisora is also a graduate of Finchley ABC and is indebted to the club for his own development and the way it helped him fall for the fight game.

Back in 2007, as Anthony watched the boxers, including Ben, spar and work out, he too was gradually bitten by the boxing bug. On his way home from the club he would often practise his own moves in the street with Ben and then continue alone in front of a mirror in his bedroom. All of a sudden, the lad who had become lost had something to focus on, something that was more powerful than the streets – and something that had claimed him. After a few visits to the Finchley club, he plucked up courage to ask trainer Sean Murphy if he could put on some pads for a workout. Sean agreed, and took him on the pads, little expecting the boy to have so much power that his hand would sting for hours after just one punch.

Sean could see that Anthony was big and strong but had been surprised by the force the lad had produced with no previous training or learning. Sean's fellow trainer at the club, John Oliver, witnessed the punch and explained why it had hurt, and why it had surprised both him and Sean so much. 'The thing with pad work is you do get problems with new boys,' Oliver told *Sportsmail*. 'They might hit on the edge of the pad and it bends your fingers. But not this boy who had come in – he hit the pad perfectly in the middle with one of his first shots, bang. Sean starts yelling and this big lad is following him, saying, "Sorry,

sorry". We were all laughing but then Sean has to go off to hospital so that's a bit more serious.

'My God, when we hear back from him it turns out he hasn't broken his hand – he's shattered it. Every single metacarpal was smashed, maybe broken in 10 places. Well, I'm 72, and I've been in rooms with Muhammad Ali and Mike Tyson – I don't think I've ever heard something like that. Even now, 10 years on, Sean has problems with that hand.'

And Sean himself still remembers the incident as if it were yesterday – hardly surprising, given he had broken his wrist and needed a bone graft. He told ITV, 'I was padding him like I normally do on a session but because he's so tall, I had to hold my hands up really high and he hit the top of the pad and bent my wrist back. I've taught the boys not to show any pain so I just cracked on but I was in agony thinking I was going to pass out. So not only has he left an impression on me — he also left a scar on me.'

It is now a legendary tale in the making of AJ the world champion, highlighting as it does the boy's determination to make something of himself and to escape his difficult youth, while also pinpointing the natural strength and ability that would enable him to do so. In 2017, when Anthony had beaten Klitschko, he would buy Sean Murphy a brand-new BMW 3-series car as a thank you for his care and guidance over the years – and for not complaining too much about that hand-shattering incident! Sean was almost lost for words as the big man handed him the keys to the £65,000 personalised motor. In a brilliant BBC documentary on AJ, broadcast days before his fight with Klitschko, he is seen giving the keys to a stunned Sean. And AJ revealed why he had bought it, saying, 'When I was younger I was partying, I was getting in trouble, I had the court cases. This was the time I thought, "What will I do with myself?" I'd found boxing while on bail and I had the opportunity to go to Vegas to fight. So I told my site manager I would go to Vegas and be back in two weeks.

'He said, "Nah, if you're not here someone else can take your job. You choose what you want to do'. So, I ended up going to Vegas. I was f****d before boxing. That was my reckless days when I was smoking. Boxing really helped me get on the straight and narrow. It was at my first boxing club where I learned discipline. How to forget your ego and listen to instructions if you want to achieve things. Sean would say, "Shut up, get on the bags, stop talking". He told me to stay focused. These guys will always have their door open for me, no matter what. I'll never forget who has been there when no one was.'

Sean Murphy eventually recovered enough to thank his protégé for the car, which even had a personalised number plate. He said, 'F*** off! Seriously? I'll be scared to drive it. I remember Josh telling me a long time ago, "I'll look after you." But him just winning a world title is enough for me. I can't believe it, it's too nice, thank you. Inside I am jumping up and down.'

Sean added, 'Josh hasn't ever seen me speechless but I was dumbfounded. He did it for me as he was in a little bit of trouble when he started here, he had an electronic tag when he first came to us, so this gave him a focus in life, he found something that he enjoyed and that he was good at.'

This was a side to Anthony's character that would make him the People's Boxer in the UK as he broke through. In the ring, he was deadly, but outside he had the kind of warm, generous and magnetic personality that brought to mind Frank Bruno, who also came to be so loved by Britain as a whole, not just in boxing circles. Anthony would be seen to be generous and kind and approachable – another aspect of his redemption from the days when he was 'a bad lad'. After presenting the BMW's keys to Sean, AJ explained how important loyalty was to him by adding, 'When it's all said and done, I never forget the people who were there for me when no one else was.'

His cousin Ben had set him on the path to boxing and would come to his rescue a second time when Anthony decided he would like to learn to box. Ben lent him £25 to buy his first pair of boxing boots and was well impressed by what he saw as AJ worked out in them: 'He took to it so naturally. But I'll always remember one of his first sessions – he was so knackered he had to wait 15 minutes before getting in the car. Then as soon as he got home he threw up everywhere. You could see, though, that he was getting into it.'

Sean admitted that AJ was older than most of the boys who came to Finchley, but that he made up for the lost years with a determination to reach the top quickly and a willingness to learn. He was inquisitive and would constantly ask his trainers why he was being told to try different moves and how they would benefit him when he had his first bout. And it helped, of course, that he was grateful to Sean and his fellow trainers for spending time with him. It meant a lot to a boy who had felt lost and unsure of the direction life was taking him. Now he knew exactly what his role in life was to be, and exactly where he was heading, how to get there and who would help him on the journey. The instruction handed out at Finchley would eventually come to be worth millions of pounds. Anthony's desire and search for perfection has also been key: it meant he was willing to put in the extra hours working on his jab, his hooks and his footwork. He has a superb boxing technique and it is all down to the effort he put in at Finchley, and continues to put in now with Rob McCracken in Sheffield.

He has great humility for an elite sportsman. Never does he think he has cracked it, and that there is nothing to learn. Sure, he is confident of his own ability – and some may call that super-confidence arrogance – but he remains willing to learn and to listen. Otherwise, why would McCracken bother to continue coaching him? If there was nothing to add to his talents, he may as well coach himself.

Sean Murphy believed he had found a raw diamond in the 6-foot-6-inch boxer. He was confident he would soon have the power to be able to look after himself in bouts and liked it that the boy was willing to take his suggestions on board. Sean decided it would speed up AJ's development if he also saw how the pros worked – so he took him along to pro gyms to spar.

It worked. Sometimes the pro sessions were bruising but Anthony learned quickly how to defend and shield himself – he had to if he were to avoid still worse punishment. Then, he learned the timing of attack – when he should throw a jab, when a hook and when not to telegraph a move so that he could launch a hammer blow. It was all coming together for the boy from Watford. With Sean's help, he would soon be ready for his first amateur bout. He was patient but wanted to get into the ring to prove to himself that he could be a decent boxer; that he *was* a decent boxer.

His first fight came in November 2008, against Nathan Brede at the Boston Arms pub in Tufnell Park, North London. Anthony took the fight to his opponent, and won. Kerry Duffy from *Boxing News* was one of the lucky few to witness AJ's debut and enjoyed the bout. In what is now accepted to be the legendary first article about Anthony, Kerry commented, 'Not to be outdone by the preceding bouts, the seniors produced several thrilling displays, none more so than Finchley's Anthony Joshua, who on his debut left the ring to a new set of fans after stopping his opponent, Minateur's Nathan Brede in the first round. The 18-year-old used his considerable 6'6" frame to maximum effect as he twice forced his man to a standing count before the referee came between them.'

And there it was. Even in his first-ever fight Anthony Joshua showed he had the knockout touch. All those fights that would follow his move to the professional arena would see him dispose of opponents within a couple of rounds, and here he was giving the earliest possible indication of his love of getting the fight over with quickly and with the minimum of fuss.

The boy who would become a phenomenon had always had the dynamite fists and determination to beat whoever was put in front of him, whatever the level and wherever the bout. The fight may have been staged in a small, sweaty boozer, but he had delivered in front of a crowd 'in the backroom of a pub'. Even back then, he was clearly ambitious to get somewhere fast – as his first opponent would no doubt testify after that first-round stoppage. It may have been a far cry from the O2, but it was so important in AJ's career. That first win gave him the confidence to believe that he could progress, that he could carve out a career for himself and that he might even one day make it to an Olympics, where he would represent his country.

Within two years of his debut, he had proved just what a prospect he was by winning the Haringey Boxing Cup in 2009 and 2010.

Anthony entered his 20s winning all of his 18 fights at amateur level, including the Senior ABA championships in 2010. Typically, he won the crown via a first-round knockout, with the Isle of Man's Dominic Winrow the victim. He had a chance to turn pro – and was offered £50,000 to do so – but turned it down as he wanted to have a stab at Olympics glory at London 2012. Anthony says on his official website, anthonyjoshua.com, that 'winning medals was much more important to him than winning money'.

Also in 2010, he became Champion of Great Britain, defeating Amin Isa. The win earned him his position as number one in the Plus 91kg weight category and meant he was promoted to Team GB. In 2011, Anthony retained his ABA title and reached the quarter-finals of the European Championships in Turkey, where he was knocked out by Mihai Nistor. The Romanian remains the only man to have KO'd AJ, but their relative fortunes since that bout would suggest it was something of a freak outcome. Just before Anthony's monster fight with Klitschko, it was revealed that Nistor struggles to make £1,000 a month and relies on funding from his nation's army to continue his career.

But the Romanian showed his humility by revealing that he did not rate himself as a boxer, and would always remember the night he beat a future world champion. He told the BBC, 'It was a special day, my trainer told me not to worry, Joshua is big but he'll go down quickly if you punch him correctly. I didn't know who he was or what he was going to become, he was a good boxer, he was moving all the time and he had a strong punch. I beat him in 2011 and in 2012 he was an Olympic champion. I am not too talented. But I love combat and I like to work . . . hard work, hard work, hard work.'

Anthony was gutted by the defeat. He believed he could have continued but instead of sulking he put all his efforts into preparing for the World Championships, which could provide him with a ticket for London 2012. He did well at the Worlds, defeating the Olympic and two-time world champion Roberto Cammarelle in the quarter-finals.

Anthony went on to win silver at the tournament in Azerbaijan, and his success secured him qualification for Team GB's boxing squad in London 2012. He had lost in the final in Baku to the host nation's Magomedrasul Majidov by one point, 22–21. It was a painful loss, coming as it did on the back of the defeat by Nistor, but that double anguish would serve as inspiration: he had no wish to go through the same emotions again.

He admitted that the defeat had left him in tears, telling the *Guardian*, 'Majidov was an unbelievable fighter. But I had only been boxing for two and a half years then because my first amateur fight was in November 2008. So he was much more experienced. Majidov wasn't big or tough-looking. I thought I would have him easy. But in the first round I was like a novice, missing shots, spinning off. I still thought it was going to be easy. But he came steaming out in the second and caught me with a beautiful shot. Boom. I was OK but I thought: "You want to take it there? Suits me." I lost my composure and went toe-to-toe with him. That cost me the fight. He won 21–20. I shed a tear afterwards.'

We have already touched on AJ's unfortunate temporary return to the wrong side of the tracks during his early boxing career. It is enough to say that he realised the error of his ways and was grateful when he was given another chance with Team GB. He had been suspended from the team after he was arrested for possession of cannabis with intent to supply, although the intent to supply charge was dropped. But he got a reprieve and made a vow to his mum that it was the end of the downward spiral, and that from now on he would stay permanently on the straight and narrow. From late 2011 onwards, there would be no turning back – and no more run-ins with the law.

The turnaround in Anthony's fortunes was apparent by the end of 2011. A year that had started with him fearing a jail term and missing out on the Olympics ended in triumph as he was named 'Amateur Boxer of the Year' by the Boxing Writers' Club of Great Britain. He would now go on to star for Team GB at the Olympics, and would eventually end his amateur career with a record that read 40 wins and 3 defeats. One of those losses he would put right when he became a professional and stopped Dillian Whyte, who had beaten him in an amateur bout back in 2009. Whyte remains the only Briton to have beaten Anthony at any level, but he found himself outclassed when they put on the gloves at the O2 in December 2015. More on that revenge match in a later chapter.

Anthony was now heading for the Olympics in London. Could he win gold on home territory? Or would the pressure of being a local boy weigh heavy? We were about to find out, at the ExCeL Arena . . .

CHAPTER 3

LONDON CALLING

As the days counted down towards the London Olympics Anthony felt a knot of excitement and anticipation in his stomach. He had certainly come a long way in those four years since putting on the gloves for the first time, and now he could see a truly tangible reward looming if all went to plan. He remained confident that he would end up among the medals but, being AJ, that was only the long-range aim: he wanted, and was working towards, the gold. Never a boy to settle for second best when he set his mind to something, he trained like a demon and maintained the belief that he would emerge triumphant in the battle to become super-heavyweight champion. It was not an ego trip as he saw it, more a rightful end product after all the work he had put into it. All the early-morning runs, the pain in the gym, the hours and hours of sparring – why would he have gone through all of that just to be happy to have participated?

No, as always, Anthony was only interested in the top prize. That was his mindset as London 2012 loomed; super-confident, but not arrogant, determined, but not obsessed, and giving 100 per cent in training, but not to the extent that he would have nothing left in the tank when the competition finally began.

Anthony Joshua was a winner, pure and simple. He went into every bout expecting to win, knowing he had done everything in his power to achieve that ambition, and his optimistic outlook meant that he had the mental strength to back up his ever more powerful physique. Those long hours with the GB boxing team trainers at the Sheffield Institute of Sport had paid off. Anthony was a different man from the one who had tentatively sparred for the first time back in 2008. Gone was the callow youth; in his place was a formidable, super-fit athlete, who would become even more powerful as the years rolled on. The evolution of Anthony Joshua, boxing golden boy, was well under way by the time of the Olympics that glorious summer of 2012.

Anthony would be the first to doff his cap and admit that he owed a hell of a lot to one man, in particular, as he went for gold: Rob McCracken, the supremo of GB Boxing and, ultimately, the man who would work for him, training him and encouraging him in his corner as his full-time coach during that super-fight with Wladimir Klitschko almost five years later. As GB Boxing's Performance Director Rob had worked miracles even prior to the Olympics. It was down to his efforts, his vision and his belief that Great Britain could reign supreme once again in the annals of amateur boxing, that the country would end up with three champions during the event. And that was a considerable achievement, given that three years previously he had taken over a squad that was in disarray and with extremely low morale, having left the World Championships in Milan with zero success. No medals and no hope.

That was all about to change under McCracken's brilliant, sometimes belligerent guidance. The has-beens would be shaken up and knocked into shape, the end result being the golds that Anthony, Nicola Adams and Luke Campbell would win in London. It helped, of course, that Rob knew about the art of boxing from his own experiences at the coalface – he himself had turned pro in 1991 in the Light-Middleweight division and, three years later, won the British title by outpointing Andy Till. In November 1995, he moved up to Middleweight and won the Commonwealth title by outpointing Canadian southpaw Fitzgerald Bruney. Eventually, he had so much success that he was considered the Number One challenger in the WBC rankings. Rob retired from the ring with a record of 33 wins and 2 losses, including 19 knockouts.

All this meant that he knew what he was talking about as head coach of the Olympics team and, just as importantly, the boxers under his command knew what he was talking about given his background, experience and record as a boxer. He had been there and done it, and had the T-shirt to prove it after fighting his way through so many bouts himself over an educational decade. As he would tell BBC Sport, 'Dedication and discipline are keys to producing a tremendous boxer, regardless of what talent he or she has got. But you learn from your mistakes and every mistake I made I pass on to the boxers and make sure they don't do it.'

It wasn't just the training and sparring, though. McCracken

revolutionised GB Boxing with many other innovations, including concentrating on nutritional and medical well-being, as he explained: 'My job was to get the right team in place, bring more coaches in, more support staff, which means we can have more boxers training with us. We've embraced sports science. The first thing I did when I came in was let these people practise their techniques, crack on with what they're trained in. If a fighter doesn't make it, they've only got themselves to blame. They're full-time athletes, everything is catered for on the medical and nutritional side, they're told what to do when they go home. They get every chance to succeed.'

This advanced approach was music to Anthony's ears. He loved innovation and anything 'hi-tech' that could help raise his own game – as we will note in a later chapter about how he set up his own specialist team when he turned professional. Anthony knew at once that McCracken could bring that extra edge to his boxing; that this was a man who could indeed take him to the next level, with his team of strength coaches, nutritionists, physios and performance analysts, and he was delighted that Rob was to be his Olympics supremo.

In 2011, Rob told the press how the build-up to the Olympics was panning out. He admitted he was pleased with the way Anthony and the others were working towards their goal and how they were coping with changes in the rules and his innovations at the Sheffield centre of excellence. He said, 'In terms of preparation, the big improvements I've seen are in the way the squads have adapted to international boxing: to the new scoring system and the change to 3x3 rounds. They are very professional for youngsters. They have travelled the world and are not fazed by anything. I'm very pleased with the way the boxers are developing.'

Anthony received an early Christmas present at the start of December 2011, when it was announced he had made the cut for London 2012 and would be part of the Olympics squad. It was a massive achievement, and he had celebrated by first telling his beloved mum, Yeta, and enjoying a cup of tea with her. Then it was down to London and the Olympic Stadium to pose for pictures for the next morning's sport back pages of the national papers, and to give his views on how he saw the bouts panning out for the GB hopefuls. Anthony was one of five boxers who had been officially selected for the London Games after sealing their qualification at the World Championships in Baku, Azerbaijan, in October. The others were flyweight Andrew Selby, bantamweight Luke Campbell, light welterweight Tom Stalker and welterweight Fred Evans. Anthony told reporters how effective the Sheffield centre had been in helping him make the Olympics cut. He said: 'GB Boxing have got a lot of Lottery funding now. They've got coaches there, they've also got a nutritionist, a psychologist, a physiotherapist and I think we're being very well prepared. Behind the fists, there is a lot of science. It's about leaving no strand unturned and going in there with every advantage. It just makes you so much more difficult to beat if you can do that.'

Rob McCracken congratulated the famous five, saying, 'Since I took over as Performance Director in November 2009, the GB Boxing squad has performed consistently well at major championships. To secure five Olympic qualifiers at our first opportunity was very satisfying and a great achievement by the boxers who have all worked hard to secure this once-in-a-lifetime opportunity to compete at a home Olympics. The five boxers are all a credit to the squad and if they box to their full potential then every one of them has the talent and ability to do well and secure a medal.'

Matt Holt, the Programme Director for GB Boxing, was also confident of success, saying, 'We're in a great place. The successes that we've had across the three major championships this year have been absolutely fantastic. At the men's Europeans we put two of our boxers on the gold medal podium and they both qualified for the Olympic Games. In Baku, we had three boxers get to the final, which has never been done collectively by GB boxers before, so that was fantastic, too. We were a little bit disappointed that one of those silvers wasn't converted into gold, but that's what we'll be hoping to do in London.'

The Sheffield centre had been a definite plus point as Anthony now fine-tuned his work there. It was plush and modern; a dream for kids like AJ who had been used to rough-and-ready boxing gyms and slumming it in B&B accommodation when training. Now they could train and develop in world-class surroundings with world-class facilities. Rob McCracken would later say it 'covers everything including medical issues and physio, strength and conditioning, nutrition, psychology, lifestyle and performance analysis and has been a massive factor in our success, giving our boxers a performance edge over their opponents.'

The £1million state-of-the-art, purpose-built boxing gym opened in 2009 and would prove so positive for Anthony as an ideal working environment that he would use it even when he turned pro and won his world heavyweight titles, returning 'home' to enjoy the facilities that had helped him win gold in 2012.

An indication of its quality came a year after its official opening when the USA Boxing squad paid a visit. They had heard all about what was on offer but wanted to see for themselves if the hype was truly justified. They soon found that it not only was, but that it exceeded expectations and was, as the press would have it, 'a knockout'. Ed Weichers, Head Coach for the USA's boxing association, told reporters, 'We have been training for the Atlantic Cup in London but really we were interested in the English Institute of Sport in Sheffield. We know that if we're going to have competitions in the UK we will be welcome to use this facility.

'The venue is very impressive, they have everything we have. I love the utilisation of space with the number of bags and rings. They have some highly technological advances in terms of video review and they've got a newly appointed Performance Director in Rob McCracken who comes highly recommended. I think BABA is really on the right track and we're trying to do the same over in the US.

'When the England team came over they were very focused, very disciplined, and competed tenaciously and they did very well. They won many more than they lost which speaks very highly of their programme. Sharing information and sharing ideas, concepts and dreams are just going to make all the athletes better. I've learnt a lot since I've been here and I'm going to learn a lot more during the rest of my stay. I think there's a lot of respect and admiration for one another and just good healthy competition which is what it's all about right now.'

Rob McCracken did indeed come 'highly recommended' and would once again prove that he was not a man who simply rested on his laurels when he encouraged yet more innovation to help Anthony and his fellow boxers the year prior to the Olympics. In 2011, it was revealed that the Sheffield centre was using a hi-tech 'video capture' system, the iBoxer, to give the boxers an additional insight into how they could improve performance. The system used a series of cameras to monitor boxers' movements in the ring, which were fed directly to a series of touchscreen monitors in the gym. The athletes could then go over the footage between bouts in order to analyse and improve performance, define fight strategy and gain a better understanding of their opponents' tactics.

Professor Steve Haake, director of Sheffield Hallam University's Centre for Sports Engineering Research (CSER), a UK Sport innovation partner, explained just how it was working in training – and how it would, it was hoped, help the boxers at London 2012. He said, 'Once the athlete has completed a three-minute sparring round or training session they can come out of the ring and get immediate video feedback on the aspects important to the session. The iBoxer system also stores the judges' scores and videos for thousands of bouts, which can easily be searched using a laptop or touchscreen PC.'

GB Boxing's full-time performance analyst, Robert Gibson, had trialled the system with the Olympic squad at Sheffield and could see benefits. He said, 'Some of the things we're looking at are to do with points-scoring dynamics. Where are points scored during a bout? What are the current gold medallists doing? What are we doing compared to them? Then we look at punch efficiency. How many punches were thrown per point? And if a point isn't scored why not?'

And McCracken was similarly effusive, saying, 'Performance analysis is an important part of our boxers' preparations. It provides us with insight on their opponents' strengths and weaknesses and, by providing them with this knowledge, builds confidence. The iBoxer system has supplemented our work in this area and enhanced the quality of our performance analysis.'

So it was little surprise that the system, developed by researchers at CSER in conjunction with the English Institute of Sport (EIS), won the Best New Sports Technology category in the MBNA Northern Sports Awards that year. It was certainly making an impression upon the boxers and trainers as they prepared for the Games. Another example of how McCracken was using technology to get the best out of Anthony and his team-mates – it was a hell of a long way on from the archetypal image of boxers working in rundown spit-'n'-sawdust gyms, spitting blood in buckets and shivering in the cold, as exemplified by the Sylvester Stallone *Rocky* movies!

As Dr Scott Drawer, Head of Research and Innovation at UK Sport, summed up, 'Our work sets out to help our athletes and their coaches learn faster than their international opposition, and this is a great example of where increasing knowledge and understanding of the sport can give our athletes a real performance edge.'

Everything was being done to boost performance and help Britain's elite amateur boxers hit optimum form just when the Olympics came around. There could be no excuses for total failure; not when so much money, time and effort had been thrown at the cause. Optimum body conditioning was key for Anthony. He had never carried any extra pounds but now he would become even leaner and meaner under the auspices of the Sheffield nutritional team. Like the other boxers, his food for each day's training was pre-prepared and left in the gym fridge in an individual food box. It was carefully planned to give him maximum strength but to keep his weight at the right level too, a balanced mix of carbohydrates and protein as; he told the *Guardian* in July 2012, 'I've just got to take it home and eat it . . . I'll get some fresh meat, fresh fish, fresh salmon, maybe some potatoes. It's important to stay close to my best fighting weight, even at super-heavyweight. My best is around 106.5kg. At the minute, I'm at 107.1kg. I wouldn't want to be, like, 109kg. After competition you lose a lot of weight, sweating and so forth. I could weigh in after a fight at 104kg. If I sat back, that's losing energy. So I have a shake, something to eat, put the energy back in. It's all about smaller portions, no carbs at night.'

He and the other boxers stayed in flats close to the centre from Monday to Thursday as they prepared for the Games. Anthony would even return to the same accommodation when he turned pro – he admitted it was what he needed to keep his mind on the job. Not spartan, but certainly not luxury, the accommodation was modest and humble – just as he liked it before a fight. Plus, of course, he was near the gym and the facilities of GB Boxing. Back in the build-up to 2012, he and the team would then train at home over the weekend, while ensuring they had regular, and much-needed, rest periods. Good sleep was especially important to Anthony. He admitted he loved taking naps to recharge his batteries and considered them an important part of his overall lifestyle and training structure. He also made sure he saw pals and family as the Games got ever closer; he loved taking time out to smile and laugh with those closest to him. Never one for seeing a glass half empty, Anthony liked to live life and to enjoy it. Sure, he knew he had to put in the long hours and hard work while training but time out was also vital – as the Sheffield centre's physiologist Laura Needham would point out in 2016. She told the *Daily Telegraph*, 'Sleep is so important for recovery. We spend a third of our lives doing it and yet we devote so little attention to it. Take napping during the day, for instance. We like our boxers to nap either for 30 or 90 minutes. If they wake up after an hour, they are likely to be in the deepest part of sleep.'

McCracken knew that the smallest improvement could prove key at the Olympics and so he was also open to the idea of pro boxers helping out. To that end he enlisted the aid of one of the very best, Nottingham's IBF super-middleweight world champion Carl Froch. Rob was Froch's trainer as well as being the Sheffield supremo and was delighted that Carl felt able to put the home nation's ten boxing hopes through their paces. 'He trains with the squad, he joins in some sessions and he spars with some of them,' McCracken said. 'It is great for his speed and tempo, and it is great for them to do three or four rounds with him, he gets them to where they need to get. He has rubbed off on them a lot and I think they have rubbed off on him in some ways as well. I know he is coming down to London and he is really keen to see them do well because a lot of them are his friends as well, and hopefully they can push on and get the medals they thoroughly deserve.'

In June, just a month before the opening ceremony, the final boxing squad for the Olympics was named and Anthony and the team posed for another photo opportunity and a further question-and-answer session with the press. He said he was very confident that the team would do well and that there was a strong possibility that they would make the nation proud. 'I think we can all go to the Games and achieve something great and bring boxing back up to where it used to be,' he said. 'We've had enough of bad decisions and fights outside the ring and all that stuff. I'm glad to be in this position but at the same time I'm not trying to be flash or cocky. I'm just trying to help put boxing back in a good place, and I think I'm part of a team that can do it.'

Every member of the group was a Games debutant but Anthony insisted they could beat the three-medal haul from Beijing 2008 – one gold and two bronze – and even equal the five-gong haul from Melbourne in 1956, when Britain came second to only the Soviet Union with two golds, a silver and two bronzes. He added, 'Five medals is a tough ask but I think we've got the talent in this team to match it or even beat it. I don't think the records are going to stop there. This team can keep getting better and better.'

The final teams looked like this:

Men: Anthony Joshua (super-heavyweight), Anthony Ogogo (middleweight), Andrew Selby (flyweight), Luke Campbell (bantamweight), Josh Taylor (lightweight), Thomas Stalker (light welterweight), Fred Evans (welterweight).

Women: Nicola Adams (flyweight), Natasha Jonas (lightweight), Savannah Marshall (middleweight).

And boxing promoter Frank Warren was convinced that Anthony would win a medal and that doing so would open doors for him to become a wanted man in the pro world afterwards. He told the *Sun*, 'If London super-heavyweight Joshua wins gold he will be the hottest property in world boxing. Four years ago he had not even laced on a pair of boxing gloves but now he is one of the favourites to capture the top prize. Joshua, 22, had a fantastic World Championships beating reigning Olympic and double world champion Roberto Cammarelle and just lost out in the final to the home boxer Magomedrasul Medhidov in Azerbaijan. Standing at 6 foot 6 inches, supremely athletic with fast hands and feet, a big punch and a million-dollar smile, he is one of the faces of London 2012. Joshua will get a medal and I expect him to be in the final.'

As an interesting tangent, it was claimed in Nigeria that Anthony had wanted to represent the African country in 2012, given his Nigerian family connections – but that he was refused a spot in the team! The claims surfaced in Nigeria and were given credence by former Nigerian national boxing coach Obisia Nwankpa. The story goes that Anthony contacted the Nigeria Boxing Board of Control 'about flying the Green and White' at London 2012 and was 'duly communicated by the authorities to join a national trial camp...but then there was a glitch.'

'This was in 2011. Nothing was heard from the boxer; who was relatively new on the scene at the time, until the end of the camp,' Obisia told brila.net. 'Eventually, when he resurfaced again, there was nothing anybody could do about it. We already shortlisted the boxers for the Games and could not drop anybody for him, he should have been at the trials. There was no way we could have put his name on the list without participating at the trial, because everybody we selected took part.'

And in 2017, just days before AJ's battle against Klitschko Obisia remained unapologetic about rejecting the champion back in 2012. He said, 'I would do it again because we must always do the things the right way.' No one connected with the Joshua camp would confirm or deny the story, but I am tempted to believe that AJ wanted to represent GB in 2012. He had put all his time and efforts into his work at the Sheffield centre of excellence and had been trained by GB coaches, so it made little sense to suggest that he suddenly had decided to opt out to represent another country, however much Nigeria remained close to his heart.

And, as the Quartz Africa website, which also ran the story, pointed out, it would be an unusual move given the quality of training and facilities Anthony enjoyed in Sheffield, as opposed to those in Nigeria which, it claims, would not be as good, 'With hindsight, it's difficult to say if Joshua would have done as well if he'd been representing Nigeria but history suggests that would not be the case. Over the years, several home-grown athletes have switched allegiances citing poor management and sub-par training facilities. Francis Obikwelu, the current European 100 metres record-holder, switched allegiance to Portugal after Nigeria's athletics federation neglected to cover medical bills for an injury sustained while representing Nigeria at the 2000 Olympics.

'It's not just a Nigerian thing either. At the 2016 Olympics in Rio, at least 30 Kenyan-born athletes represented other countries. Similarly, half of Bahrain's Olympic track and field team was almost entirely made up of Africans.'

Still, it offered yet another talking point in the ever developing narrative of a boxer who would be on the brink of becoming a star if he could shine at London 2012.

In another encounter just before the Olympics, Anthony crossed paths for the first time with someone who would become a good friend. Little wonder, perhaps, given that Troy Deeney, Premier League goalscoring machine, was also from Watford, as well as playing for the town's football club. Troy had popped into a barber's shop in the town for a quick haircut and Anthony was already in the chair. The duo struck up an unlikely conversation after Troy noticed that Anthony was eating as he had his hair cut.

Troy told the *Daily Mirror*, 'I first came across Josh before he was an Olympic champion. I walked into a barber's in Market Street, in Watford town centre, and he was in the chair. I noticed he had his food with him, and I thought it was a bit unusual to be eating while he was getting his hair cut, so I asked him, "What's for lunch?" He explained he was a boxer who was going to represent Britain at the Olympics, and was going to run the five miles home, so he was just putting some fuel in the tank. I thought, "Fair play to you." We just got talking. It was never a case of, "Ooh, you're a boxer! Can I be your mate?" None of that s***. I just respected he was working hard towards a goal, and every conversation we've had since then has been straight down the barrel, no grey areas, no bull.'

Their friendship would be put on hold when Troy was jailed for three months for affray, in the summer of 2012 – the very time when Anthony was going for gold in London. 'I was locked up when he fought at the Olympics,' Troy added. 'But

I was banging on my cell door when he won the gold medal.' They have since revived their friendship and Troy admits he is 'proud' to know Anthony, whom he calls a 'role model'. They have much in common, both growing up in a tough area and both taking some hard knocks and making some bad mistakes along the way. But, ultimately, both have worked hard to put the past behind them and make amends with the way they now live their lives and by offering their help freely for charities and worthy causes.

After his unexpected meeting with Troy Deeney, Anthony became one extremely busy young man. The Games were almost upon him and he and his team-mates set up camp at the Olympic Village in Stratford, East London, on 24 July. They were undoubtedly surprised, if nonetheless delighted, by the welcome they received. No one had anticipated that the London Olympics would be the massive morale booster for the nation that they would turn out to be – but the omens were good that Friday, as Anthony and the GB team attended a welcoming ceremony after 'booking' into their accommodation.

Anthony told friends he was happy with his quarters. He was rooming with fellow GB boxer and the team skipper, Tom Stalker, and they spent some time acquainting themselves with the set-up and amenities. The village's 2,818 flats had been fitted out to cater for 16,000 athletes and officials from 200 countries; it was reported that, among much else, it had needed 11,000 sofas, 170,000 coat hangers and 5,000 toilet brushes. And, given just how large an area the village covered, it was hardly surprising that a few athletes struggled to find their way back to their accommodation that first night!

Earlier, they had been greeted by a troupe of jesters and the Deputy Prime Minister, Nick Clegg, although he denied he was part of the troupe. Joshua's team-mate, Anthony Ogogo, spoke for the group when he said that he had enjoyed the welcome ceremony, which also included performers on stilts and cycles singing to Queen's 'I Want To Ride My Bicycle'. Ogogo said. 'It was amazing. It's hard to explain quite what this feels like, but it's exactly as I expected it would be as a kid. It's weird walking around here with so many strangers seeing you in the tracksuit and just saying "Well done". I can't wait until my first fight on Saturday to do my thing.'

Mr Clegg believed it was the prelude to a successful Games, telling BBC News: 'This Olympic Village is a triumph and I've already spoken to some of the athletes, who've said the facilities are the best they've ever seen. No doubt there will be a few ups and downs along the way but I think people are going to be so proud that Britain has been able to put on such a successful Olympics. This isn't just about the athletes, it's about the nation really coming together to support Team GB. This is the greatest show on the planet and I'm clear that the nation is going to love every minute.'

He would be proved emphatically correct in that assumption as the nation got behind the Games. They would prove to be something of a rallying call; harking back to a time when Britain had been truly great, after four tough years for the many in the wake of the financial crisis of 2008. Back in Fleet Street, we who had followed Anthony's progress intently, and sensed he was something special, were now about to find out just how good he actually was – and whether he could justify the hype and the growing belief that he was a boxing great in the making. Could he follow in the footsteps of Audley Harrison and Lennox Lewis? Or would it all end in disappointment; a crushing anti-climax? The eyes of a nation fixed on the young man from Watford, whose destiny was undeniably – and literally – in his own hands.

CHAPTER 4

THE GOLDEN BOY

Anthony had enjoyed the welcoming ceremony at the Athletes' Village and was seen smiling and laughing as he walked with his GB colleagues into the Olympic Stadium before the opening ceremony. But then it was time to hit the serious button again and to re-focus on the job in hand. If he were to be successful – as in winning a medal – he knew he would have to remain at his peak physically and mentally. Striking gold would entail coming out on top in four testing fights and, for all his bulked-up physique and unquestionable strength, fitness and speed of hands and mind, he was still an outside bet to win the competition. He remained something of a novice; he lacked the experience of many of the boxers in the tournament and many commentators predicted that his wily, competition-hardened rivals would have the edge on him. But they had not counted on Anthony's tremendous will to win, or the fact that he was sharper than his rivals and that he had a home crowd roaring him on every step of the way at London's ExCeL Arena in Docklands.

As if to stress how he would need the public's support, beating even his first-round opponent was a tough ask. Anthony was drawn against the impressive Cuban boxer Erislandy Savon, a typical example of the consistently excellent amateur-boxer production line developed in Cuba. He was fast, tough and certainly not a stepping-stone first opponent for Anthony. He also came from good boxing stock – his uncle, Felix, won three Olympic gold medals and six world titles. So it would take all the boy's talent to keep Savon at bay, and then to get the better of him.

There was a glimmer of hope in that Erislandy had been stopped by Azerbaijan's Magomedrasul Medzhidov in the World Championship quarter-finals the previous year – while Anthony had only lost by a single point to the same opponent in the final. And GB podium coach Dave Alloway, while admitting that Savon would be a tough cookie, also insisted that Anthony, for all his inexperience, was more than capable of holding his own. He told reporters the boy's training and talent meant he could achieve great things, 'He will take it as it comes against the Cuban. You have to beat the best to be the best, and the Olympic Games is always going to be a tough tournament, but this team has faced the best around the world and are now used to taking who they get in the draw – whatever the event.'

GB team manager Matt Holt backed up that sentiment, saying, 'Anthony had a fantastic world championships and he is ready for the fight. It is always tough against the Cubans, but Joshua can mix it with the very best.'

Anthony did just that, emerging victorious against Savon, although it was a close call. Indeed, many commentators believed that the Englishman was outpointed by the Cuban – and that he only got the verdict because he was part of the home nation, with a noisy home crowd behind him. The *Sun's* veteran boxing correspondent, Colin Hart, led the naysayers, insisting, 'There is little doubt he was the beneficiary of a blatant hometown decision in his first bout. He was clearly outpointed by Cuban Erislandy Savon, who was much faster and more skilful.' On the other side of the coin, the *Guardian's* Kevin Mitchell dubbed such suggestions 'ludicrous' and said Anthony 'was through on merit'.

Many readers of the national press tended, perhaps surprisingly, to agree with Hart and with Jeff Powell of the *Daily Mail*, who also argued that 'Joshua was outboxed and outclassed.' But one boxing fan, from Austria, put forward a persuasive argument that Anthony had won fair and square, at the same time questioning the loyalty of the fighter's own public. The fan said, 'I do not understand why British people are so critical of their own people. There are five judges and a point is scored when three judges pressed their button to register a scoring punch, within one second of each other. A punch must land with the white part of the glove to score and land with sufficient force (the decision of the judge). Therefore since Savon was backing away most of the time, some of his punches may not be scored as they may be judged to have landed with insufficient force. As for me, I thought they landed about the same number of punches, but because Joshua applied pressure most of the time I think he deserved the win.'

That is a fair case for the defence. And, having watched the bout again, I tend to agree with it. The fight was certainly much closer than Hart and Powell suggested, and Anthony threw some awesome right-hand punches which, had they connected solidly, might even have led to a knockout. And, to be realistic, the crowd may have been partisan but the judges certainly were not – and there were five of them. They scored the fight 17–16 and that seems about right – it shows how close the bout actually was and credits both boxers. The scoring went like this: Round 1, 6–5 to Joshua; Round 2, 8–7 to Joshua; and Round 3, 4–3 to Savon.

Afterwards, Anthony – while believing he had done enough to get the nod – hinted that he was due a break from a judges' panel anyway after he lost out in the World Championships in front of a partisan crowd in Baku – where he believed he had done better than the scorecards suggested. He told reporters, 'I knew it was a close fight and I leave these things to the judges. I had the crowd against me in the World Championships in Baku when I lost the final. I must put it behind me and move on.

'It's all about staying calm. Even though it's your home crowd you get in there and you zone in on something different. The atmosphere definitely spurred me on, but I was calmer than I thought in there. The atmosphere is unbelievable out there and I have to give the crowd great respect. We were both whacking each other with shots, we kept fighting to the last bell and let the judges do the scoring. Savon is a tidy boxer, he was much more slippery than I expected. That was a good first fight and will put me in good stead for the rest.'

Anthony's next opponent was to be China's Zhilei Zhang,

who stopped Australia's Johan Linde with a big right hand in the second round of their fight. The consensus was that the Chinese was not as good as Savon, but that he could still cause Anthony problems if the latter let his guard down. He had, after all, been a silver medallist in the Olympics at Beijing four years earlier. Anthony used the few days in between the bouts wisely, training lightly, resting, then stepping up his efforts while still making sure he got enough sleep. He spent downtime relaxing with his friends and with room-mate Tom Stalker, and admitted that he was enjoying his time in the Olympic Village. He had worked hard enough to get there and his attitude was, as always, to take the positives from the situation. It gave him the chance to meet fellow world-class athletes from other countries and to see how they trained and unwound. He also enjoyed being around the GB team as a whole, not just the boxers, and was known around the Village as 'one of the really good guys' because of his 'permanent smile' and 'welcoming approach'.

Not that Zhang would recommend him as a guest for Christmas dinner after the beating AJ dished out in their big bout at the ExCeL. Again, the big Brit was backed by a sell-out, fanatical crowd who wanted to see him advance to the semis for, of course, that would mean another guaranteed medal for Team GB. If he beat Zhang, AJ would be assured of a bronze at the very least – and the already magnificent GB total medal haul would get another terrific boost.

Anthony began the fight with the crowd urging him on and their deafening support ringing in his ears. He came out with the clear intent of battering his rival into submission with a series of lightning quick jabs and hooks. Zhang was relieved to hear the bell go for the end of the first round but it was short-lived as Anthony took the fight to him again in the second. All his work was beginning to pay off and it was of little surprise when he knocked the big Chinese to the canvas with a magnificent right hook. To give Zhang his due, he proved a durable opponent, too, refusing to stay down, and he did indeed fare better in the third and final round, drawing that one on points. But he had no complaints when the final result was announced: a comfortable 15–11 victory for the British boxer, who was becoming more confident with every round and every bout. As his experience grew, so did Anthony's self-belief. He always believed before the Olympics that he could win gold; now he felt he had the proof as he ruthlessly destroyed Zhang's hopes.

After the fight Anthony declared himself happy and proud that he had secured at least a bronze medal, but made it clear that he would work hard to improve on that. He told the press, 'That medal represents a journey, a lot of hard work, but it hasn't stopped here. It is going to get tougher and I'm going to have to keep my head on my shoulders and try to change the colour of that medal. I learned so much from my first bout and I learned so much from this one too. I'm going to go away from these Olympics a new man because the experience is unbelievable – it's character building. I'm not miles better than I was when I went to the World Championships, but I have improved. It's going to be a long career and I'll never stop improving until I finish, but I'm getting better bit by bit because of the experience.

'Every fight is a learning curve for me and Lennox Lewis has advised me to use my jab more. I also know I must keep my feet on the ground.'

Those words summed up the man and the boxer that Anthony had become since he took up the sport and started to turn his life around. From a drugs rap and a prison remand, he had become a responsible, likeable, hard-working human being and a boxer who was willing to listen even as he approached the peak of his amateur career – a potential gold medal at the Olympics. Sure, he still had a self-confidence that few people have, but it did not stray into arrogance stemming from an unpleasant ego-mania. All sportsmen and women who reach the top of their pile need to have that utter self-belief that they *can* achieve the impossible and that they *can* remain unbeaten. But there must also be a level of humility that enables them to take constructive criticism head on, and allows them to learn from it and move forwards – even when the criticism is the last thing they want to hear. As one well-known footballer, whom I shan't name, once said to me, 'I used to think I knew it all, that I didn't need anyone's help or advice. I liked to talk and not listen – after all, I was the big "I am". It was only when a player who had done it all told me that we are born with one mouth and two ears that I started to get the message! From then on, I tried dead hard to listen more, rabbit on less!'

Anthony Joshua had no need to learn that lesson. Since taking up boxing, he had always been more than willing to listen. He knew that if he wanted to change the direction he was heading – from a potential life of crime to one of sporting greatness – he had to be taught. A boxing source said, 'Anthony said it was like learning to drive – you couldn't just get in the car and do it, you had to be taught. Similarly, he was happy to take advice from people who had been there and done it in the boxing world and use it to be the best he could be.'

Two former GB Olympic boxers who had turned professional were also of the opinion that Anthony was on the right track for gold – and a potential goldmine of a career if he too turned pro after London 2012. Audley Harrison, who won gold at Sydney 2000, and David Price, a bronze medallist at Beijing, had signed to fight each other at Liverpool in the October after the London Olympics. But at a press conference to promote the fight a couple of days after Anthony beat Zhang, both men were keen to give their views on AJ's hopes as well as their own forthcoming duel.

Audley said, 'I rate him a lot. He is young and hasn't got a lot of experience, but what he has is tremendous ability and I'm really looking forward to him going all the way. He has a great chance of winning the gold. He's got to go out there and earn it – they're not going to give it to him – but he has a great chance. The world's at his feet. I'm going down there for the semis and the finals and I'm really looking forward to seeing our boxers perform.' While David added, 'I think Joshua's got his name on the medal – he's destined to win that medal the way things have gone with him. He's a great talent. To be an Olympian in its own right is a fantastic achievement, so to get a medal and potentially win the gold after such a short period of being a boxer, he is, without doubt, a massive talent.'

He went on to say that it was also important that Anthony and the other GB hopefuls realised the role the Sheffield centre of excellence had played in their rise: 'They've raised the bar again. They do a fantastic job up in Sheffield. I predicted three gold medals before and I stand by that prediction. To have three gold medallists would be fantastic for the sport.'

But the semi-final would be no walkover for Anthony – he

was now faced with another giant of a man, the 6-foot-9-inch van Dychko. The Kazakh fighter had beaten Germany's Erik Pfeifer and Canada's Simon Kean on his way to the semi-final. But his luck ran out when he came up against Anthony in a tough scrap, which ended 13–11 in AJ's favour. The Brit had employed a surprise secret weapon before locking horns with the much more experienced Dychko – he shadow boxed with Lennox Lewis and listened as the great man offered him some advice on how to deal with his man-mountain opponent. It proved sound advice indeed as the British fighter weathered the storm that saw both men exchanging powerful blows before Anthony's proved the stronger and he came out on top.

The fight was scored 8–8 at the end of the second before Anthony emerged looking for the kill in the final round. He threw some brilliant heavy punches at his opponent, leaving him with a bloody nose and a deflated look at the end. AJ's left jab had proved to be a key weapon and he was improving with every bout. It was no longer a pipe dream that he could bring the gold home for his country – now everyone associated with or interested in British boxing, officials and fans alike, was beginning to believe that it was a realistic eventuality. Now he was assured of at least the silver.

'I knew he was going to be awkward and that I had to adapt,' Anthony said after his victory. 'Lennox Lewis gave me lots of advice – he told me to back this big guy up with my jab. I also did some shadow boxing with him after Nicola Adams had won her gold medal. I feel I'm getting better but I'm still learning. The job's not done yet. I want that gold medal. I believe I can get it and then we'll see what the future holds.

'For now, I have just got to stay calm. That's all I keep telling myself. I'm still a day away from gold. It is not just about me. I know I have got my family at home, my coaches at Finchley ABC, the friends up there and everyone buzzing. It's a team achievement and I am just happy I can make everyone smile.'

Even the vanquished Dychko had nothing but praise for his conqueror. He said, 'Anthony is a very good boxer and I am happy with my bronze medal.'

The fans were quick to applaud AJ for his win – and for his unflashy attitude. One said, 'What a humble and gracious guy this Joshua is. Not acting flashy in his interview, just getting the business done.' Another said, 'Audley Harrison must be wondering where it all went wrong watching this exciting new talent.' While another added, 'Anthony is just getting better and better. I have no doubt at all that he will win the gold medal and then go on to become the best British heavyweight of all-time!'

The last tribute was still some way from being realised in the warmth of the summer of 2012. It was certainly a hot August night when AJ lined up for the super-heavyweight final against Roberto Cammarelle, ten years his senior at 32. The experienced Italian was boxing at his third Olympics but Anthony had already beaten him 15–13 in the previous year's World Championship quarter-finals. Anthony said, 'Cammarelle is a very talented guy and he's Olympic champion. But if I continue to grow as a fighter as I have been, then hopefully I will win.'

He admitted that he had an extra spur to win the fight – he wanted to do it for his friend Tom Stalker, his room-mate in the Olympic Village, skipper of the GB Boxing Team and general inspiration to Anthony and the rest of the crew. Light welterweight Stalker lost in the quarter-final against Munkh-Erdene Uranchimeg and Anthony explained, 'I'm going for the win and I will dedicate that win to my room-mate Tom Stalker, who has kept me going since he lost.'

Tom proved what a great captain and friend he was by putting aside his own disappointment to counsel Anthony as the big man strode towards the final. They talked tactics and Tom kept Anthony's confidence sky-high and 'helped settle him' when the pressure bore down ever heavier. Anthony would be the first to admit he owed a debt to Stalker for his help at London 2012 and the two stayed good friends after the tournament. Stalker, who struck gold at the 2010 Commonwealth Games in Delhi and also won medals at both the European and World Senior events, was sure that Anthony would win the final, telling him the key was to 'stay calm and take his chances'. The Italian was a formidable opponent but so was Anthony Joshua, and Tom reckoned AJ was a more powerful puncher and that could ultimately prove decisive.

It wasn't hard to see why Anthony and Tom bonded. They had both come from the dark side of life and seen the light thanks to their boxing careers. Just as Anthony had been in trouble with the police earlier in his life, so had Tom. Yet both had pulled clear and turned their lives around after finding their salvation in the boxing ring.

Tom even started in the fight game relatively late in the day, at 17, again on a par with Anthony. He explained the turnaround in his life, telling reporters, 'I'm not the cleverest so I'm not sure if I would have held a job down – so basically boxing has saved my life. If I didn't get into boxing then I don't think I'd be the person

I am today. I don't know if I'd be in jail or not. The best thing I ever did was go into a boxing gym. Before I started boxing at the age of 17 when my girlfriend got pregnant, I was working in a Marriott hotel washing dishes for two years. I had my first fight when I was 19 and for the first year I was boxing I couldn't even throw a punch. I was terrible! That's no word of a lie – I was always awkward in the ring but I couldn't punch the pads or bag properly. I just stuck at it and got there in the end.'

Anthony was 'gutted' when Tom lost that quarter-final fight at the Olympics and it made him even more determined that he would beat his Italian opponent in one of the final events of the Games, the super-heavyweight event taking place just hours before the closing ceremony.

AJ knew it would not be easy; the Italian policeman was a tough customer who had taken few prisoners in his boxing career (although he had in his cop uniform). But Anthony felt confident as the day of the battle drew close. He was younger, and he felt he was both fitter and a better puncher. Plus, of course, he had already beaten Cammarelle, and that was an extra confidence boost and a psychological advantage. Anthony was looking forward to the fight – he knew he would have the support of most people in the stadium and that he could rely on his ever-growing band of fans to urge him on.

As he entered the ring AJ looked calm, collected and ready for action. He waved and winked to his fans and friends and looked as laid back as you could hope for. But his demeanour changed dramatically as the ref called him and Cammarelle together for a quick rules-and-etiquette rundown. Suddenly, he was the totally focused, determined mean machine that was ploughing its way through the amateur heavyweight division. Watching the fight, I had the feeling right then that this would be his day.

Yet it would be a near-run thing, a win, a gold and all the accolades to go with it, but a hell of a lot of controversy, too. From looking unbeaten at the first bell, Anthony seemed a little overawed by the occasion, which was hardly surprising for a guy of 22. But his slight indecision was seized on by the Italian, who himself now appeared full of belief when he might have feared a negative outcome against a younger, more powerful opponent.

The surprise turnaround was reflected by the fact that AJ was three points behind, and facing almost certain defeat against the reigning Olympic champion, as the fight entered the final round. But brave Anthony gave everything, managing to level the scores with a battling display. After two rounds of relative struggle, we saw the real Anthony Joshua stand up tall and be counted in the final round of the bout and of the Olympic boxing tournament for 2012. It was exciting to watch as the crowd cheered him on and a proud moment to be British as he fought his way to GB's 29th gold medal. The judges declared the result an 18–18 draw, but Anthony triumphed on the countback. The Italians were furious and protested loudly, but their claims were dismissed.

Anthony Joshua had done it: he had won an Olympic gold at 22, just four years after committing properly to boxing. It was a quite remarkable achievement, but fair reward for all the effort he had put into turning his life around and striding towards greatness. All the lonely hours in the gym, pounding the roads and living a life of abstinence and total devotion to the project had paid off. He was the king of the Olympics and the amateur world – now he was the hottest talent in boxing, a wanted man, who could choose his next move. He could continue as an amateur and aim for the next Olympics, in Rio, four years away. Or he could take a massive step and turn professional, which would offer wealth and glory at a different level. It would be a decision that Anthony would wrestle with for several months before deciding where his future lay.

For now, he simply said he felt he 'pulled it out of the bag' and that he was delighted to have won for himself and everyone involved in his development, plus his friends and family. He added, 'This is much more than a gold medal for me. It is a life experience.' He told the post-fight press conference that he had felt inspired by his favourite film, *300*: 'The moral of the film is to never give up, to never surrender and it was just like that in the third round. My legs were screaming but I just kept throwing punches, catching him with straight shots down the middle. I never panicked. Sometimes I wanted to stop but my arms were just flying. I pulled it out of the bag.

'That medal represents my journey and the support from the team. It's much more than just a gold medal, it's a life experience and I'm just proud to have it round my neck. Now I want to gain more experience and just keep on pushing. I've only had 43 bouts, I'm not in a rush to turn professional. It's never been about money. Money does help. My mum pays bills. I've got bills to pay as well, but thanks to UK Lottery sport funding, that's the most money I've seen in a long time. I'm happy with that.

'To leave the Great Britain set-up just for money would be

a big mistake. It's a great experience to be working with such great people, head coach Robert McCracken and his team. I don't want to lose that just for a bit of money thrown in my face. These memories are priceless.'

Lennox Lewis and Audley Harrison were ringside and draped the Union Jack around Anthony and themselves, with Lennox declaring, 'Josh has what it takes now to become the next heavyweight champion of the world.' It then emerged that the bookmakers William Hill had cut the odds of him achieving that to just 6–1 . . .

But for the final night of the Olympics, Anthony's only focus was letting his hair down at the closing ceremony and after-party with his fellow Team GB team-mates, in celebration of what had been a remarkable summer for him personally, for the team as a whole, and for all of Britain. Team GB had delivered 65 medals in total – the best since the first time London had hosted the Games in 1908 – and earned a remarkable third place in the medals table, above the might of the Russians. The successes of Anthony and so many other British athletes had lifted the spirits of a nation, and things would never be the same again for the boy from Watford.

That would be emphasised later in the year when he was told that he would receive an MBE in the Queen's New Year's Honours list as a reward for his efforts at the Olympics. The award capped a remarkable six months that had seen him propelled from relative obscurity, among most non-sporting Britons, to headline news. Anthony would receive his gong in February 2013, from Prince Charles at Buckingham Palace, and later told how the Prince had said to him, 'Shouldn't you be playing basketball?' – a reference to his 6-foot-6-inch frame. Anthony added, 'Last year was unbelievable, it's a great honour to have an MBE in my family.'

After the MBE ceremony, he was also asked by reporters if he could still remember every moment of the final bout that had earned him the gong. He laughed, nodded and replied, 'At the end of the second round I was three points down. I couldn't believe it, I was shocked. In the corner I said to myself, "You're three points down . . . doesn't mean you've lost this battle, you've got one round to give it everything you've got." I didn't want to turn it into a scrap so I kept on boxing. I threw my combinations of left and right and pulled it back and it went to countback, where they watch the video replay and add up all the averages and scores, and I won it by two points and became Olympic champion.'

It was a surreal finale to a seven-month period of Anthony's life that had seen him fight as a GB hopeful in the London Olympics, end the tournament as the champion and a gold medallist and finally receive an honour from the future king at Buckingham Palace, London. Not at all bad for a boy who had appeared to be heading to the wrong side of the tracks just five years previously. From a drug rap to king of the ring. It was a true story of redemption and transformation that is a credit to the boxer himself, to his brilliant GB Boxing back-up team, and to his friends and his family who had stood by him during the dark days. Anthony Joshua had become a national hero loved for his talent in the ring and for his humility as a person only too aware that he had been given a second chance.

It was further to his credit that he had not only snatched

that chance, but had thrived upon the challenge to triumph at London 2012. That was a remarkable achievement in itself, but it would actually turn out to be only the start of a journey of success that would lead him to selling 90,000 tickets for one of his fights at Wembley and becoming the best-known boxer on the planet.

CHAPTER 5

THE JOSHUA TREE (OF LIFE)

Anthony is not your typical bachelor boxer. He is a young man who believes there is a life outside the ring and outside the typical boxer's bling of say Floyd Mayweather, who is often pictured showing off with his wealth in many poses. Whereas the latter is all about cash and flash, Anthony has a variety of different interests that are much more down-to-earth and highlight his intelligence and general inquisitiveness.

He lives a relatively simple life, preferring to spend time with his mother than being out on the town with a different woman on his arm every night. He is a modern-era athlete who looks after his body and resists the temptations that lead many a man astray. OK, he was no saint in his late teens, but for how long does he have to carry the weight of those misdemeanours? He has changed, sought redemption and found it in boxing and is living a good, honest, decent life nowadays.

Anthony will be the first to tell you he missed out on a good education, hence his youthful misdemeanours. And while boxing proved a salvation, it does not define him as a person. It is his job; his way of paying the bills and ensuring his family are comfortable. Sure, he makes big money but do you ever see pictures of him in the press, splashing it around carelessly like Mayweather?

It's not for nothing that Floyd is known by the moniker 'Money'. Many fans have slammed his showing off and hedonism as 'obscene'. In May 2017, he was pictured loading $5 *million* into a car as he prepared to launch a strip club in Los Angeles. Anthony, on the other hand, recently *gave* a car to his former trainer – a brand-new, luxury BMW. Such is the difference between class and having none. Mayweather even provided an Instagram clip to give the American public a peep into how his 'gentleman's club', called 'Girl Collection' was progressing. And he made it quite clear what punters could expect when he offered dancers the chance to join him in the adventure:

> Welcome to the all-new "GIRL COLLECTION". We are an upscale, Gentleman's Club offering a great opportunity for talented dancers (both local and out of state) to dance for what is set to be the hottest Gentlemen's Club in all of Las Vegas! If you are a talented and energetic, exotic dancer looking to earn top dollar in a professional, luxurious and fun environment, then "GIRL COLLECTION" is where you need to be. Please include your best and most recent FULL BODY photos and HEADSHOT along

with a resume of your experience and or why you
should be chosen to work in our super exclusive club.
Please be sure all photos ONLY include yourself as we
are very exclusive and bare [*sic*] the right to be selective.

Now can you imagine Anthony Joshua setting up a similar
club in London? Or his mum Yeta letting him do so? This is a
boy who is grounded and who has always insisted he wants to
live 'a normal life' away from the ring. He even moved back in
with his mum after he beat Klitschko and earned an estimated
£15million. He had been living in a posh rented pad as he
prepared to do battle, not far from Yeta's former council flat in
North London. AJ bought it for her for £175,000 shortly after
turning pro in 2013, and also bought her a Range Rover car. He
is loyal to Yeta and they remain very close. He is the first to say
that she played a massive role in encouraging him to become the
best boxer on the planet, although he bans her from watching
his fights in case it upsets her.

After beating Klitschko he told reporters how his aim was
now to get away from the hype and the fury of the ring, and to
simply get back that 'normal life'. He had no plans to paint the
town red or to splash out extravagantly as Mayweather would.

No, instead he said, 'I'm a good man, I'm a family man, and I
love life. How do I plan to celebrate? Wake up midday for once.
Wake up midday and then catch up with my family. Normally
I take a holiday, but I think this time what I'm going to do is
just pop round to some of my family's house and catch up. We
spend a quarter of the year training, and then normally you go
on holiday and then straight back into training camp. I don't

want to do that, I want to catch up with family. And that's it. Go back to normal living.'

That word 'normal' again. And he wasn't using it to get the public to see him as 'a regular sort of guy', or 'a nice guy'. One of his fiercest rivals, Dillian Whyte, had called him out at a press conference prior to their December 2015 bout at the O2, claiming it was a false image Anthony was presenting to the press to try to make himself likeable. Whyte said, 'I don't like the guy because he's fake and he puts on this demeanour that he's this and he's that. That he's a good guy, but he's not really. He's a bit of a scumbag, to be honest.' Dillian was wrong, as anyone who knows Anthony will confirm. He IS a good guy and female sports journos will tell you that he is 'surprisingly gentle for a man who is a boxer' away from the ring.

He also loves spending time with his baby son, Joseph Bayley Temiloluwa Prince Joshua. Anthony adores his boy and, after a bout in April 2016, shared a snap of Joe on Instagram with the message, 'Now the dust has settled it's time to relax with my lil champ JJ.' He always calls him JJ and proudly displayed 'Joseph' and 'Angel' (his niece) on his boots during the fight with Klitschko. Anthony says of his boy, 'Boxing gave me my motivation, so having a son just keeps me on course. Everything I'm creating, I have someone to pass it down to, because I'm not going to be here forever. All the things I gain in life – wisdom, material objects – I can pass on to the heir to the throne, as such. That's a nice relationship.

'You know what I like about the kids? About JJ and my little niece? It's a time when I am so disconnected with what's happening in the world because you're in the park and you become a kid, and you focus on what they're doing. It's like going holiday – you take yourself away from the situation. When I am with my son and my nieces, I take myself away from the hustle and bustle of the world and concentrate on these kids, who haven't got a worry in the world. I've always been a family man.'

During the fight against Klitschko, his mum looked after Joe and afterwards Anthony Facetimed the tot in his dressing room at Wembley. He said the little lad was shocked by the black eye that Wladimir had inflicted upon him! 'My son JJ was with my mum while the fight was going on. I was speaking to my son who is 18 months and I could see he was looking at my eye and he went, "Wow".'

Anthony's hobbies outside the ring also portray the other side of a man that will surprise many people, who consider the average boxer to be a Neanderthal creature. Not so, AJ. No, for instance, he is one of quite few boxers who enjoy a game of chess. He learned to play the game in August 2013, saying, 'A boxing match can be a bit like chess. That's how the Cubans fight, like a game of chess. They're clever and that's what I've got to be. Before I used to rely on my strength, speed and power, now I've got to rely on my smartness.' A month later, he revealed his growing love for the game when he tweeted, 'Late night chess with my niece.' And in an accompanying Instagram picture he showed his niece Angel trying to catch him out with a clever move on the board. The picture inspired many comments from his fans, with one saying, 'Good job, this is a great way to strengthen this beautiful young one's ability to understand life is like a game of chess.'

And the following year he revealed one of his boxing heroes, the great Lennox Lewis, was the inspiration behind his taking up the game. He said, 'Lennox got it into my mind and then a friend taught me. Chess, it's the same type of thing in the ring, like taking one of your opponent's pieces and then counter-attacking. You need to be two moves ahead all the time.'

He then also tweeted that he was hoping to beat Lennox at chess. One fan commented, 'That will keep your mind sharp for boxing.' Which was exactly why he enjoyed chess; it challenged him and he liked the tactical side. Just as boxing was always about outboxing an opponent, so it was also vital to outwit them with clever moves. A surprise uppercut here, a questioning jab there and a massive right to end the contest. Check, mate.

Anthony also likes to read regularly – again, he believes it keeps his mind active and that helps translate to an active, demanding mind in the ring. He is very much of the opinion that physical, brute strength doth not a great champion make. He wants to stay at the top for a long time and to do that a boxer needs to avoid the numbing blows that slow you down. Speed of mind as well as body is a key component to achieve that aim.

He told the distinguished broadcaster Mihir Bose that the books he had enjoyed included *Think and Grow Rich*, *The Secret*, *Freakonomics* and *Rich Dad, Poor Dad* and added, 'We all have questions we want to ask about life. I want to find out about the Egyptians, their history, because they lived before us. I want to know what went on in the past.'

Of course, with titles such as *Think and Grow Rich*, *Freakonomics* and *Rich Dad, Poor Dad* commentators and, no doubt, fellow boxers, would scoff that Anthony was only interested in reading books on how to get rich quick. But that is missing the point – the three books are about much more than that. On a superficial level, money is one of the key elements in all three, but just as importantly, there is a more profound message about how to live life in a way that makes you happy. Money is a help, no doubt about it, but not every millionaire is happy and Anthony Joshua was aware enough to understand that he needed to live a fully rounded, measured lifestyle if he were to enjoy the millions he was about to make. Lennox Lewis had helped set him on this path – in Lennox he saw a bear of a man, a boxer who had done it all, won it all and who had the millions in the bank. But he also saw a man very much at peace with himself unlike, say, Mike Tyson.

Lennox was easy-going and laid back, and was a man of culture who liked chess and reading, so it was perhaps inevitable that Anthony would follow closely in his footsteps. To live like Lennox as his career progressed and then into middle-age after boxing was an admirable ambition. And if self-development books pointed the way on that journey, then Anthony was all for travelling down the road. The publishers' blurb for *Think and Grow Rich* gives an inkling of how Anthony was looking to such books to improve his life state, as well as his bank balance:

[This is] the wildly successful motivational book from personal development author, Napoleon Hill. Having sold over 30 million copies over the past 70 years alone, this ground-breaking volume reveals the secrets of hundreds of the world's most affluent people – exposing the thought-processes and success mindset that can help you too, to enjoy unlimited prosperity and abundance. The thirteen step program found in this book has everything you need to set you on the path to incredible wealth and success. Regardless of your current circumstances, education or business experience ... once you begin to read this book, you'll have access to the truths and lessons that can teach any man or woman – young or old, rich or poor – to turn their dreams for an abundant life into a reality.

With this book, the formula for everything you desire – to be applied in ALL areas of life – is in your hands. Simple, direct, but incredibly powerful too – this book has the potential to change your life for the better.

It is perhaps telling that the book was written in 1937 – Anthony, as he had claimed, was looking to the past for answers and positive direction for his future and many people had commented on amazon.com that its essence was spiritual, rather than money-oriented as you might imagine given a cursory glance to its title. As was *The Secret*, another of Anthony's favourites, written by Rhonda Byrne in 2006. As one reader commented, 'It's very good for those, who like me always think negative with no self-motivation. This book will try to kick your butt and make you think in a different way.'

Even *Freakonomics* was a read that offered much more than a get-rich-quick manual, again as the publishers were keen to point out:

Freakonomics is at the heart of everything we see and do and the subjects that bedevil us daily: from parenting to crime, sport to politics, fat to cheating, fear to traffic jams. Asking provocative and profound questions about human motivation and contemporary living and reaching some astonishing conclusions, Freakonomics will make you see the familiar world through a completely original lens.

I can imagine how the cynics will continue to scoff and laugh at this side of Anthony Joshua but surely we should be giving him credit for his attempts at self-development? After all, isn't boxing known as the noble art? Do all boxers need to live up to a stereotypical image of thugs outside the ring? Muhammad Ali, the greatest of all time, certainly did not. He was the first boxer to understand that there was a life outside the ring and that intelligence and a thirst for knowledge were commendable. Lennox and Joshua are merely followers in his gigantic footsteps.

Not for nothing does Anthony have the word 'Wisdom' tattooed on the top of his right arm, the one that usually inflicts most damage on his opponents in the ring. And, while still an amateur in 2011, he said his three desert island essentials would be, 'Books, toiletries and food' while if he wasn't a boxer, he would be 'in college studying'.

Anthony has also expressed his preference for thoughtful, progressive politicians. Donald Trump would hardly be someone he would ever back, or want to play gold with as Rory McIlroy had. No, AJ once admitted his admiration for the bombastic Trump's predecessor as US President, Barack Obama. In an interview with *Men's Health*, Joshua revealed Obama was the man he most wanted to have a drink with, 'It would be great if he could sort me out with a visa and maybe show me around the White House.' Given that admiration, it is more than likely that he will end up reading some of the ex-president's books and his thoughts on life and how to live it well.

Having set out the case for Anthony Joshua the philosopher, I should add that he is no shrinking violet outside the ring . . . as his taste in top-quality, energetic hip-hop music shows. He loves to lose himself in the beat and once admitted that 50 Cent's *Get Rich or Die Tryin'* was his favourite album! But he himself makes it clear that he has moved on from the sentiments expressed in the record, that it was an integral one in his growing up and youth, but not in the right way. He said, 'When we were younger and getting into trouble, I remember listening to the CD with one of my close friends. And it was that mentality – basically succeed or nothing. I was obviously putting that mentality in the wrong direction and maybe that's why I've done all right in boxing, because I now use it in the right way.'

Nowadays he still loves hip-hop, but in the more reflective messages of Jay Z than 50 Cent. Anthony admitted he had been inspired by Jay Z and how he conquered hip-hop both through music and business. Anthony is also drawn to grime like Stormzy, whose album *Gang Signs and Prayer* reflects the duality of black life in the UK, with everything from gang violence in London through to the power of prayer through gospel. So even within the music of one of his new favourite artists there is an undercurrent of a search for spiritual meaning mingled in with the realities of how life can be harsh and unforgiving if you take the wrong path, as Anthony himself did in his troubled youth.

He had also given a clear indication of his love for music before the fight with Eric Molina in 2016. He told *GQ* Magazine that music was 'essential to his training' and that he always wore a pair of Beats headphones by Dr Dre to enjoy the tunes he loved for workouts in the gym as he prepared for the bout. They included Stormyz's 'Scary', James Brown's 'It's A Man's, Man's, Man's World' and Emeli Sandé's 'Garden'. There were also some rather more aggressively boisterous numbers, including NWA's 'F**k Da Police' and The Notorious B.I.G.'s 'My Downfall'.

Anthony has lifted yet another award, this time *GQ*'s Sportsman of the Year gong, and it was not just because of his talent in the boxing ring but also as a result of his personality and ability to attract interest outside boxing. Like Muhammad Ali, he was reaching an audience away from the knockouts, such was his charisma and charm. He even admitted to *GQ* that he *didn't* want to be viewed purely as a boxer, telling the magazine, 'At the moment, I still think of myself as a man who fights. My mind-set at the moment is that I don't want the sport to consume me or define me, because when it comes to an end I worry that I won't be able to come to terms with life without boxing. But I am working towards changing that. I am a boxer and I want to be the world's greatest fighter, but I am not there yet because of my attitude. The mentality I have at the moment is that I am just an ordinary guy, I feel humble when people want to meet me, take a picture with me, all of that stuff. I don't take it for granted because deep down it doesn't make sense to me. I mean, at my last weigh-in two women fainted. How mad is that?'

Stormzy would actually accompany AJ into the ring at the O2 before his clash with Dillian Whyte. For the fight with Klitschko, Anthony walked to the ring accompanied by 'They Ain't Ready' by Skrapz, then 'Seven Nation Army' by the White Stripes and, finally, 'Juicy' by Notorious B.I.G. Meanwhile, Wladimir proved that it wasn't just the new kids on the block who could get down and with it as the old-timer emerged to the sound of two of his own favourite artists, the Red Hot Chilli Peppers and Puff Daddy. Of course, Klitschko himself was hardly your traditional boxer; he enjoyed the arts and the finer things in life away from the ring and was engaged to the bubbly actress Hayden Panettiere. She is also an activist who has battled to save the whales, to stop dolphins being hunted and to use education to reduce teenage pregnancies. Clearly her determination to fight for what she believes rubbed off on Klitschko. In 2013, he joined her in Kiev in the Ukraine for demos against the country's decision to opt for closer economic ties with Russia rather than the EU. It was also a demo against a corrupt government's stripping away of people's rights 'to protest, speak and think freely and to act peacefully without the threat of punishment'. Hayden explained why she and Wladimir had joined the rally, telling reporters, 'The fact that freedom of choice, freedom of opinion is even a question is ridiculous. They are doing this peacefully, which I am all for. They are saying all they want and at the same time they are peaceful. It's uneasy. I have a lot of respect for people who come out for what they believe in.'

Wladimir echoed her words as they stood in the square, backing his brother and fellow former heavyweight boxing world champion, Vitali. The latter had left the ring and become an opposition politician in his Ukrainian homeland, and was at the forefront of the anti-government protests.

Clearly, both Klitschko brothers are, like Anthony, a formidable mix of brains and brawn. Like Ali, they had become spokesmen of their generation for their own downtrodden people. It helped explain why he got on so well with Wladimir – they had much in common. A love of boxing as an art, for sure, but also that inner desire to widen their sphere of knowledge. It was admirable that AJ was keen to follow in the path of such exemplary, humane boxers. Fighters who had a conscience and who wanted to help their fellow man. As AJ would say, again and again, he had no desire to be defined simply by his career in the ring. Anthony wanted to have something to fall back on when his career was over – maybe he would help other youngsters, like himself, who had also taken the wrong path find ultimate redemption. He certainly spent a lot of time educating himself through reading and learning about the world outside boxing. When young boxing hopefuls asked for his help, he always reminded them that it was important to have a life away from the ring. That you couldn't box for ever, there would come a day when you were too old and when someone else would step into your shoes. So have something else to fall back on for when that day arrived; whatever your outside interests, they would occupy your mind, and that was key. It was good advice from someone who had wisdom tattooed on his arm, but also in his heart and mind.

CHAPTER 6

ANT AND DECKED

'He's a nice guy outside the ring – but a nasty
motherf***er inside it'
– SEAN MURPHY, ANTHONY'S FIRST TRAINER

In the end, it would be a decision forged after months of agonising – but, precisely because of that period of contemplation, he was sure it was the right one. Anthony would turn professional and joined Eddie Hearn's Matchroom Sport organisation on 11 July 2013, in preparation for his first pro fight. Eddie would be his promoter but would also become a close friend and someone he could confide in. Anthony had won gold at the London Olympics some 11 months earlier, and had debated long and hard whether to stay on the amateur circuit, with a guaranteed £50,000 a year from Team GB, or branch out and join the pro ranks. The money would be much bigger as a pro, assuming he was successful, as would the profile he would command both at home and internationally. By turning pro, Anthony literally had the world in his hands. It was logically the next move, but he had felt a bond and a loyalty to Team GB, and especially his brilliant trainer, Rob McCracken. But he had to look after his own future. He was a latecomer to the sport and was pushing 24, so it was the right time to earn the bucks. And, in a clever twist to the tale, he would employ McCracken as his pro coach, while also permitting him to continue to head up the Team GB outfit.

So, through tactical thinking, AJ had reached the ideal situation and everyone was happy, from McCracken, to Team GB, to Eddie Hearn, who had captured the golden goose every promoter was after. My friend Pat Sheehan, the *Sun's* boxing correspondent, summed up what many in the boxing world were thinking as details of the four-year deal were, not surprisingly, not made public, '...after talking to all the major promoters, it is understood Joshua accepted less money with Matchroom because his fights will be aired on Sky Sports. He was forced to delay his decision to move into the paid ranks as he needed delicate surgery to repair ankle damage shortly after the Games. Joshua joins the same stable as fellow Olympians Tom Stalker and Luke Campbell, who makes his pro debut in home town Hull next Saturday. They were part of the hugely successful 10-strong GB boxing team at the London Games and both were awarded MBE's by the Queens for winning gold medals. Joshua is the fourth to move to the paid ranks from the 2012 GB squad.'

My information was that Pat had hit the nail on the head. That AJ had joined up with Eddie because he liked him and because he felt at home with him. Plus the carrot of the Sky TV link was a mighty one if he were to quickly increase his public standing. It would enable him to become an easily recognisable name and face than if he had signed for more cash with someone who had no TV contract.

The board of the British amateur boxing association was disappointed to lose Anthony but philosophical about it. BABA chief executive Matthew Holt said: 'While we would have liked Anthony to stay for Rio 2016, his achievement in winning gold at London was something very special and we recognise his wish to pursue other opportunities and challenges. Like others who have represented their country superbly in recent years, Anthony will remain part of the GB boxing family and he will always receive a warm welcome at our training facility in Sheffield.'

That was another definite plus for AJ for he would take up the offer and spend weeks up at Sheffield preparing for his pro fights. He loved working at the centre of excellence as it provided all he needed for perfect preparation. Facilities for boxers were brilliant and the accommodation was basic but ideal in his eyes.

Boxing fans were also impressed with the set-up and felt AJ would be a big success in the pro fight game. One said, 'It's great news that Joshua is going pro and that he is signing with the Hearn organisation. He's on a winner already because he'll be featured on the telly with the bouts that Sky show. I reckon he'll go on to become one of the best British boxers ever and will surely win a world title.' While another fan said, 'If you're competing with the best in the world at amateur level, you've got a good chance of doing it as a pro. Even Audley [Harrison] had a world title fight. Joshua only started boxing when he was 18 so he's on a steep learning curve, but if he's managed well to begin with, I'd back him to go all the way.' And yet another added, 'Joshua can go on to do well as a pro. The

UK Amateur game is in trouble right now with the ruling authorities and it's time to move on. I think he's done the right thing at the right time. Hearn will move him slowly but correctly. Good luck to him.'

Eddie had taken many boxers to the top of the pile and considered how best to move Anthony's career on. Obviously, it would have been foolhardy to throw him in at the deep end. He would start off slowly and work his way up through ever tougher rivals until, hopefully, the time would be right to take a world title shot.

Anthony made his professional debut at the O2 Arena in London on 5 October 2013, as he took on Italian Emanuele Leo. Ironically, his last amateur bout had been also been against an Italian in the London Olympics final the previous year. Then, he had beaten reigning champion Roberto Cammarelle to win the gold medal. Leo was recognised as a journeyman, even though he had an impressive record of eight wins out of eight fights.

He had provided problems for previous opponents in that he was a big man and had dubbed himself, 'The Colossus of Copertino'. But at 32, how would he cope against the raw aggression of Joshua, who was almost a decade younger?

They would battle for supremacy over six three-minute rounds rather than the traditional four that Anthony could have expected as a debut pro boxer.

The low-key nature of the rival put before him meant AJ would not be the headline act at the O2 – that privilege would go to Scott Quigg, in a WBA super-bantamweight title fight against the Cuban Yoandris Salinas. At a press conference to announce the fight in September 2013, Anthony further elaborated about why he had taken so long in coming to a final decision about turning professional, how he remained torn over whether to stay in the GB Olympic squad and his decision to join the Hearn camp. He said, 'The main thing was how to structure my improvement, my training, stepping away from the Great Britain team, which had developed me in just 16 months from being ranked 46 in the world to Number 1. I wanted to continue that progress. I thought, "If I turn professional, am I just going to end up training in a garage somewhere in London, with someone who doesn't know much about me – or shall I stay in the Olympic team and continue to develop?"

'I changed commercial agencies and took time to speak to a lot of people. In all that time, I was having meetings with different promoters, different trainers, lawyers. So, when I turned professional, I was in a better position than most pros signing their first contract.'

The fight against Leo provided a gentle run-out for Anthony as he dispensed with the Italian in less than three minutes. He was naturally enough pleased with the first-round knockout but was wise enough to admit that much sterner tests awaited. Leo looked a tad flabby and unfit, and AJ floored him with a powerful right to end the contest. 'There were big expectations on me as people wanted to see what I've been up to in the 14 months I've been away,' he told BBC Radio 5 live. 'I had to stay relaxed. I've been doing a lot of work outside of the ring in the gym and I feel like I showed bits and pieces of my skills tonight. Everyone is proud and hopefully everyone can understand what my dreams are. I just need to stay disciplined, focused and hopefully everyone will support me and let me crack on with it. Then you will see the best of me.'

Anthony later told the *Sun* he was delighted with the support fans and family gave him against Leo, 'I'm a London boy and it was really good because I had all my family and friends as well people who had come from across Britain there to support me. What makes that special was I put on a good show for them all to see. Having so many people there to support me doing what I do for the first time since the Olympics made it a really good time.'

Eddie Hearn's plan was to try to settle AJ into the pro arena as quickly and as comfortably as possible – and the project demanded that Anthony take *three* fights before the end of the year. Leo was the first and just three weeks later he would be pitched against fellow English heavyweight Paul Butlin in Sheffield. He was confident he would have no problem beating Butlin as easily as he had beaten Leo, saying, 'Not to sound cocky or anything, but I'm going to win. I train hard, I'm really focused and I'm determined. I'm sure he is as well and I've watched him time and time again on YouTube. I don't like to judge my opponents from what I see, but I think I know the key to beat him.'

To his credit, Butlin lasted a round longer than Leo, with the ref stepping in to award victory to Anthony via a technical knockout. Heavily tattooed Butlin was 37 and had shown considerable courage in trying to carry on the fight after he was struck by a series of powerful blows, finally falling to a stunning one–two. And AJ paid tribute to his opponent after the fight, saying, 'I'm still improving, still cracking on, but it's always good to get a win. Butlin is a tough guy. I like someone who comes to fight, who is game, and that's what he did. Boxing isn't complicated – you've got two arms and you've got to find a way to knock them out.'

It was good to hear his basic philosophy on boxing at this stage of his career – use your arms and knock 'em out! Anthony was keeping it simple as he found his way and, clearly, it was working. But he would have to develop more detailed, tactical plans and approaches if and when he fought the likes of Klitschko. The Ukrainian was a master of timing and ring craft; Anthony would uncover similar skills and mind-sets as his own pro career developed. For now, he was a mere toddler whereas Klitschko was a war-weary veteran.

Eddie Hearn was delighted at how his boy had come through another pro fight unscathed, telling Sky Sports that the defeat of Butlin should not be dismissed as a formality, given Paul's record, 'Anthony showed so much more composure tonight. Butlin is a seasoned pro who went the distant twice with Dereck Chisora. This is a different class we are talking about right here. People talk about we've got to take him at the right pace, but that's going to be very difficult to do.'

Next up, just 19 days later was Croatian battler Hrvoje Kisicek in one of AJ's favourite venues, the legendary boxing arena that was York Hall in Bethnal Green, East London. Kisicek did not enjoy his view of the surroundings as much, going the way of Paul Butlin in that he also was demolished in the second round. Once again, the ref had to step in to stop Anthony's opponent suffering more serious damage. It was the boy's third bout in little more than a month – and all three had seen him triumph with plenty left in the tank. Former world heavyweight champion Larry Holmes and current British and Commonwealth title holder David Price were among interested spectators ringside.

There was some criticism amid the growing acclaim for Anthony and the way he had started his pro career. It was suggested by some pundits that the men being put before him were not up to standard; that, OK, it was sensible to start off with boxers who wouldn't knock him out, but Kisicek, like Leo, did not look in top condition. Some critics moaned that they were flabby and should not have been in the same ring as the Olympic champion.

Ian Wright, the former Arsenal footballer, joined the chorus of disapproval, tweeting, 'Love Anthony Joshua. But at least get him someone who's in shape. What's he learnt from that? Pointless.' He would then add, 'No one expects him to go in with seasoned pros yet. Just fitter looking fighters. C'mon.'

Most fans agreed with Ian, with one saying, 'This was like watching a big bully beat up a little fat kid. He needs better opposition if he's going to learn anything from these early fights.' Another continued the criticism, adding, 'A second-round stoppage of who? When will feeding canvas-backs to up-and-coming boxers stop in this country? They learn nothing from it and gain a sense of being much better than they really are until they meet a middle of the road American – or a hungry Mexican from the same weight division and are found out to be well short of the mark. Give them fights that test them – it's called sorting the wheat from the chaff. No disrespect to this young fighter but he learned absolutely nothing from this foray into the ring other than his opponent's manager gave not a fig for his boxer's welfare or health!'

But some fans urged patience, pointing out that even the most fearsome boxers of previous era had been introduced in a similar way. One boxing fan argued, 'To those slating the standard of Joshua's opponents so far, just look at Mike Tyson's early years. Like Joshua, he was fighting every couple of weeks against fairly no-mark opponents and it didn't do him any harm. Eddie Hearn is just trying to nurture Joshua right now and build up the guy's confidence. There's no point rushing things and potentially ruining a promising talent, especially when he's only three fights in. The harder opponents will come in due time but, for now, enjoy the KOs.'

Anthony heard the criticisms: he was only human. But he explained that no fight was a foregone conclusion – that it just took one punch and one lowering of defences and you were in trouble, even if you had won Olympic gold. And he felt the fights were helping him develop, 'I worked on a few things in there. He was cagey, awkward and durable. It's important to work on things in the gym and take that to the ring.'

After the flurry of initial bouts, Anthony would now take a break from the ring for a couple of months, enjoying Christmas and New Year with his family and then hitting the gym hard for a couple of fights in February and March, 2014. First up on 1 February was Welshman Dorian Darch, another win within two rounds, this time in Cardiff, and then it was off to Scotland for a clash with Argentine Hector Avila a month later. A huge left ended Avila's trip in agony. At least AJ was showing what he could do around the whole of the UK, and the Glaswegian crowd were as happy as anyone to see the Olympic champion in action. He had fought four pro fights and his record was 100 per cent victories, and all within two rounds.

The start of his pro career could not have gone any better, although the whispers continued: when would he fight someone who could take him beyond say six rounds? But it was hardly Anthony's fault that he was so powerful a puncher – when Mike Tyson was knocking people out quickly at the start of his career the main reactions were gasps of admiration about the man's brutality and about 'what a fighter he was', not moans and groans about the bouts lasting less than five rounds.

The swift knockouts would continue. At the end of May, 2014, Anthony would take on Matt Legg in London. It was his Wembley debut, on the undercard of the Carl Froch v George Groves fight, and it, unsurprisingly, did not last long. Legg was beaten by a right uppercut after a mere 83 seconds of the first round. AJ then took his roadshow to Liverpool in what was expected to be his first real test, as he came up against former British champion, Matt Skelton.

Skelton did not do his hopes any good by saying he believed Anthony was another Audley Harrison – essentially an Olympic champ who could not cut it at the highest level in the pro world. Skelton found that not to be the case as he was stopped 27 seconds before the end of the second round. A few days after the fight, Skelton, to his credit, admitted he had got it wrong. Skelton told *Bedford Today*, 'I thought we would go the distance but he was so much physically stronger than we thought on the inside. I can't take anything away from him and he looks like he could be a world champion with that strength.

The first round we were OK, he caught me with some good shots so we were happy. I don't think he is another Audley, he seems so much more hungrier and fresh so he has the ability to achieve much more.'

Joshua was knocking his opponents over like skittles in a bowling alley. None had gone more than two rounds in the seven out of seven pro fights he had now won. But on 13 September 2014, an opponent went three rounds – although he was dropped and stopped in the third. Step forward the brave Kazakh boxer Konstantin Airich, who tried to make a fight of it as AJ headed up to Manchester on the latest leg of his UK tour.

Just over a year after his first pro fight at the O2 Arena Anthony headed back to the Greenwich venue for a battle that would bring him a title – against Denis Bakhtov for the WBC international heavyweight crown. The Russian had previously not been beaten inside four rounds but was leaning on the ropes, struggling, from the middle of the first round. The referee stepped in to stop him suffering further punishment a minute into Round Two. 'I really enjoyed it,' Anthony told Sky Sports after the fight. 'It's time to step it up, that's where the spitefulness is coming in. I just wanted to hurt him. I wanted to box, I just wanted to see what he could take. He was a strong guy, I just wanted to make light work of him.'

Eddie Hearn was also chuffed at the way AJ had gone about his business to win the title, 'That was phenomenal. He gets better and better. He is such a down-to-earth guy, a role model for young people. This is a great opportunity for British boxing, to have somebody like Anthony Joshua. He is going to go through absolutely everybody in the heavyweight division. He can be as humble as he likes. I won't be. This is the most special fighter I have seen in a long time. He is going to clear out the entire heavyweight division and unify it. This is phase two and, by the end of phase two, he will be top 15 in the WBC. Every ranking body is going to want him in their rankings because he is an absolute superstar, not just of boxing, of sport.'

Anthony told reporters that he was ready for 'phase two', and that everything was going to plan, 'One step at a time. This is phase two. In year one, we went from Emanuele Leo to Mr Bakhtov for the international title. Phase two, you can kind of see what route we are going in. Michael Sprott is first and, by the end of it. I'm sure we will be fighting for another belt or some sort of British title. That's what I'm looking forward to already. I have to go back to the changing room now and do about 20 minutes of pad work because I was scheduled for 10 rounds and only went two, so I've got to make up the rest!'

The last part of his comments was interesting and showed he and his team were meticulous in their planning. As yet another fight had ended swiftly, Anthony would do enough pad work afterwards to cover ten rounds, rather than the two. Of course, it wouldn't be as realistic and effective as a fight over ten rounds but it would build up his stamina for the time when that happened. It was a clever, intelligent move and typical of the groundwork Team AJ put in in their bid to take him to the pinnacle of the sport.

Just one month on from the title win over Bakhtov, Anthony began Phase Two with that bout against Sprott. He and the team headed back up the motorway to Liverpool but the British title eliminator against the ex-Commonwealth champion lasted just

86 seconds, in yet another first-round demolition. Once again, the ref had to step in to save a rival from further pain.

The victory had been swift and again the doubters voiced their opinions that AJ was being fed a diet of has-beens and won't bes. But there was significance to the win – as Hearn now told the boxing world that Anthony would soon take on a man who no one could dismiss as easy meat. Kevin Johnson was a tough American who had gone 12 rounds with Vitali Klitschko and Tyson Fury and would provide Anthony with a considerable challenge. Hearn told reporters, 'We will take on Johnson in the New Year and Anthony will be ready to face anyone in the country next summer. When he backs you onto the ropes he's ruthless.' Anthony added: 'Johnson is durable and he's got a lot of experience and quite a lot of mouth, so it should be a fun one.'

Meanwhile, IBF and WBA world super-middleweight champion Carl Froch, who was also in Hearn's stable, made it clear he believed AJ had done well to dispose of Sprott. Carl told the press, 'I know Anthony very well, he'll go on to win world titles. Michael is nearing the end of his career, but when's the last time you saw such a specimen in the heavyweight division as Anthony? He unloads so impressively and tenaciously, it's perfect. Matching him up is a nightmare. Everyone loves him and rightly so. What a fine fighter and person he is, he's the full package.'

It was a lovely compliment from a man who should know what it takes to make a world champion, and who had quickly become one of Anthony's biggest fans because of the talent and likeability we often talk about.

But before that big clash with Johnson, Anthony had to take care of two other bruisers. All three fights, including the Johnson one, would take place in a two-month spell beginning at the start of April and concluding at the end of May in 2015. Remarkably, considering the challenge Johnson was expected to provide, young Anthony would beat all three fighters in a total of seven rounds. It was testament to his ability and self-belief that he could finish off guys who knew their way around the professional venues much better than him in such an unflinchingly powerful manner.

On 4 April, he travelled to Newcastle for the first of the three fights, against another American, Jason Gavern. Gavern was punched to the canvas four times as Anthony laid into him. The ref stepped in to end the punishment in Round 3. To be fair to Jason, he had taken the fight at short notice (only a week) and admitted a certain fight at the prospect of meeting AJ in the ring. They had previously sparred and, in a remarkable admission to *Boxing News*, he outlined how he anticipated further heavy punishment, 'Back in August of last year, I was in camp with him for 10 days. I guess we did around 12 or 15 rounds together. He's so heavy-handed. Sparring with him sucked, I'm not going to lie to you. I was sore, my body hurt. Every time he hit me it hurt, and that was with bigger gloves on. Now I've got to fight him with smaller gloves! Oh my God.'

Jason also outlined how much he respected and liked Anthony as a person and how the Englishman had been keen to ask him questions and learn what he could from the veteran American's experiences.

Given how the two men got on well, it was lucky that Gavern

faced Joshua at a time when he was returning from a five-week layoff from a stress fracture in his back. He was perhaps a little ring rusty. God knows how Gavern would have coped if he had been the second of Anthony's three victims in that two-month spell!

AJ admitted at the post-fight press conference that he had not been at his best, saying, 'I had a bit of ring rust so couldn't display everything I have been doing in the gym. But once the momentum gets going I will be able to display some more shots, some more sharp shooting. I have boxed in Glasgow, Manchester, Liverpool, London and I have to say Newcastle is right up there with the crowd. There are a lot of expectations and Jason is a very awkward opponent. He's a slippery customer and he is there to make me look back and he did a good job of that. I have a job to do and that is get a win. If I can start pushing to British titles, European titles step by step these fights won't really mean anything when I am experienced and a champion.'

The next man to face the sledgehammer was Brazilian boxer Raphael Zumbano Love, in Birmingham. Anthony ended the contest against the 34-year-old with a second-round right-hander that floored Love. More significantly, Kevin Johnson was ringside watching the fight and saw for himself the challenge Anthony would present to him when they touched gloves at the end of the month. Johnson entered the ring and posed for a picture with Hearn and Joshua before both fighters spoke about their impending bout. Anthony smiled and was as confident as ever when he said, 'I'm feeling more confident with every fight and looking forward to fighting this man. I don't mind how many rounds Kevin and I last in London as long as we put on a good show for the fight.'

Meanwhile, Johnson, a decade his elder, made the mistake of saying he expected an 'easy' fight at the O2. He had also claimed that Anthony was 'a media hype job' and that he had not had a proper test yet but that he, Johnson, would not only provide that test but would destroy him, too. They were the sort of comments sure to wind Anthony up and in that sense were foolish and incendiary. Johnson had never been stopped before and that had perhaps lulled him into a false sense of security. If so, it would be a blunder he would forever regret – a blunder, in fact, that would have him announcing his retirement soon after the fight.

Anthony took him out in front of a delirious crowd at the O2 in just 4 minutes 22 seconds. The man who was going to deliver a crushing defeat was himself crushed in just two rounds. AJ later said, 'This shows I have the power but there were times when I was on the inside that I could have been more explosive. So far so good, but in the back of my mind I know it's going to get tougher. I'm going to stick with the people who have guided me to this point rather than fall into somebody else's hands who thinks I'm the finished article.'

He added that the O2 was becoming like a second home to him – clearly it was his favourite venue. He liked the crowd being close by and the way they backed him, constantly urging him on to glory. Anthony said, 'I have travelled about so many places with Matchroom but the O2 is my home and it is filling up more and more every time. This is what I am here to do. My coach really drills me in the gym and it is only right the hard work pays off. People say that guy will test me, this guy will test me. It is only going to get tougher and I will fight tougher opponents. The game doesn't stop.'

While Eddie Hearn believed the O2 crowd had witnessed the future of heavyweight boxing, in the way that Anthony had brutally ended Johnson's career. Eddie added, 'That was devastating. We witnessed the future heavyweight champion of the world. We have to do things right and we will progress him at the right pace. He is a great fighter and he is British. We will fill this place again. This guy is going to beat every single heavyweight in the world. We have a chance for a heavyweight to fly the flag for Great Britain and let's all enjoy the journey of Anthony Joshua.'

For Johnson, there was only despair and shattered pride, although the fat paycheck for a swift night's work may have held some consolation. Back in the States, he would eventually give a valedictory speech in which he claimed he was finished as a fighter and had the good grace to congratulate and praise his victor – the young Englishman who had certainly shocked him. Johnson would still sound a little dazed and confused from his bruising encounter, saying, 'Young kid, strong kid. It just makes you evaluate. When it's your time, it's your time. I think it's my time to get out of the game. That's it for me. I'm not playing. I'm not going to sit back and stay around and suffer losses to the young fighters when I'm a seasoned fighter. When you experience a loss like that it's time to get out of the game. Joshua is a young kid, a strong kid. I look forward to watching him on the big screen as he goes on the climb the rankings. I can't really comment on his power because I had to take it. Had he known that I couldn't block any of his left hooks, he would have knocked me out with a left hook. I couldn't even put my hand up. So that's it. All I could do was bend over to my right and hope he doesn't throw that many hooks and his arm gets tired, but it's time to get out of the sport for me.'

That was the point at which Anthony Joshua had arrived – after just 13 professional fights. He had forced a redoubtable boxer into considering retirement, such was his power and brutal determination to achieve an early KO. Johnson would, like many boxers who could not resist returning when it was clear time was against them, ultimately not stick to his decision. As this book went to the printers, he had taken another two fights, the first against Jamal Woods, which he won, but the second, up against Kubrat Pulev, would end in defeat.

But he would not forget the defeat in his 37th pro bout at the hands of Joshua. It had left him on the brink of packing in the fight game and he would certainly not be seeking a rematch against AJ.

Ironically, two years earlier, there had been a similar fight with a similar outcome and a similar reckoning, with both boxers being inextricably linked to Anthony Joshua. One of the fighters contemplated retirement after the thorough beating he took at the hands of the other. Only on this occasion, the defeated boxer, Britain's Audley Harrison, would go through with his threat and quit the fight game after coming up against the top-notch American fighter, Deontay Wilder.

Harrison, like Anthony, had been a gold medallist at the Olympics and was something of an inspiration in that AJ thought if Audley could turn pro and make a fist of it, so could he leave the amateurs and give it a go. While Wilder remains the man most likely, along with possibly Tyson Fury, to ask more questions of Joshua than any others. Audley suffered a KO at the hands of Wilder in Sheffield. It was Wilder's British debut but it did not last long – the official time of stoppage was 1:22 of the first round. Four days after the fight, Harrison announced he was considering retirement at the age of 41, telling reporters, 'I've got to be realistic, it's looking like it could be the end. It took me a lot of fortitude and persistence to get back to this position and it's going to be hard to come back from here. I felt sharp and comfortable in there but he caught me with a big shot. I took a knee and he was still throwing punches. I wanted to continue, I had my senses about me. This one is going to be a hard one for me to take.'

He then finally conceded enough was enough, putting out a statement to explain why it was all over: 'I am no longer a professional boxer, and that is good with me. After locking myself away for the last five weeks, I've tried to focus and turn back the clock to get myself into fighting condition. I've also seen specialists for my brain, eyes and various other experts to test my body functions in regards to strength, power, speed, reaction time, cognitive function and agility.

'Additionally, I looked at the latest research into concussions and traumatic brain injuries (TBI). After years of denial and sticking to my guns, I'm finally getting out of my own way.

'I've suffered a few TBIs and will have to work hard to reverse some of the effects taking punches to the head has brought about to my overall health. I have vision problems, vestibular issues that lead to balance disturbances, and have serious bouts of irritability and moodiness that comes with TBI recovery.'

It was sad to hear of Audley's health struggles – for all those who said he crumbled at the first sign of heavy pressure, he had clearly taken more pain that those critics imagined. He had also helped many young British boxers believe they could successfully forge a path from the amateurs to the pros, including Anthony Joshua, who continued to speak of Audley with respect.

And, of course, his gold medal win at the Sydney Olympics paved the way for the likes of AJ, Luke Campbell and Nicola Adams to follow in his footsteps – it convinced the Olympics board to plough more funds into backing Anthony and Co so they could have more chance of being similarly successful.

Audley bowed out having lost seven of his 38 pro fights since winning that Olympic title back in 2000.

Unlike Audley, Kevin Johnson would still be under the illusion that he could return and defy time.

For Anthony, the future was bright, for Audley it had become brighter, but for Johnson it was worrying, probably most for his family. The victory over Johnson also marked Anthony's first defence of the WBC international heavyweight title he earned with the win over Denis Bakhtov the previous year.

It was 13 pro fights, 13 Kos, 13 wins now; a perfect record. But it was also time to up the ante, to pit him against some much tougher opponents. The next three fights Eddie Hearn set up would give the camp a much clearer idea of where exactly their man stood at that moment in time. They would take place over the next seven months and, on paper at least, AJ would have to be at his very best to come through all three unscathed. It was an exciting time in his career, he had fought many boxers who, while not journeymen, were not going to be aiming for a world title shot. Now the opponents would be tougher, have something to prove, would not be happy to simply take home a paycheck and would have their own intense motivations to push Anthony to the limit. Their aim was to take him on and beat him. Each was a proud man and each believed they could leave the ring with a victory, let alone surviving more than three rounds. If the 'Phase Two' sequence AJ and Eddie spoke about had begun with the bout against Johnson, who had certainly been expected to put up a much stiffer resistance, it was now moving into a much higher gear.

The three men contracted to provide a fair yardstick of Anthony's progress were Gary Cornish, Dillian Whyte and Charles Martin. The Whyte bout caught the imagination, dubbed as it was as a 'grudge match', the Martin fight would give Joshua a chance to win his first world heavyweight title as a pro and the Cornish scrap pitted AJ against the Commonwealth title holder and an extremely tough Scottish fighter. Anthony was especially looking forward to the Whyte bout as it was the first chance he had to avenge the loss he suffered to the Brixton battler when both fought as pros. He also did not like Whyte very much; the two men were polar opposites. Whyte was brash and liked to indulge in street insults while Joshua was more measured and tried not to lose his rag. However, it would be a fight that saw him do just that, as he went toe to toe with Dillian, and later admitted he had 'lost it' to some extent.

The Martin fight saw him come up against an American whose real quality was something of the unknown. Martin had won the IBF heavyweight crown by default in many people's eyes. It had been relinquished by Tyson Fury and Martin 'earned' it by beating Vyacheslav Glazkov, lifting the vacant title with a technical knockout after the Ukrainian had to stop with a knee injury in the third round. It meant Martin held the crown without really proving he was a king. Sure, he had thrown some fairly heavy punches, but the calibre of Glazkov was also unknown. He would probably have gone the way of most of Anthony's other opponents, in less than three rounds, had the two men ever fought.

Of course, after his victory Martin, a 29-year-old southpaw, claimed he felt he had deserved victory and that he now planned to rule by winning all the world heavyweight belts. Even from his cameo against Glazkov, it was difficult to visualise him beating his fellow American, the fearsome Deontay Wilder, the WBC holder, let alone Anthony Joshua. But Martin told the assembled press corps that was his aim, however delusional it may have been. He said, 'I want to unify the titles – I want to fight, I have not had a fight tonight. I am sorry for him, it is unfortunate he was unable to finish the fight. It was meant to be. We had 12 rounds and I was pacing myself. I was going to pick it up as I went along. I didn't even get what he was doing. He was scared. You could see it in his eyes. I still wanted to fight. It's 12 rounds, that's what I trained for.'

Glazkov, a 2008 Olympic super heavyweight bronze medalist, had been tipped to win the bout as he was much the more decorated of the two fighters. He was unhappy at the outcome and felt that Martin was not a worthy holder of the belt. He was the favourite going into the fight having fought much tougher opponents and wanted a rematch when he was fit again. Glazkov said, 'This should have been my belt. I already had him figured out. I slipped and I felt a sharp pain in my right knee and I felt it give out. I'm very upset. I want a rematch when I recover.'

That rematch would never materialise. Martin, as the champion, would go up against Joshua and that would be the end of the argument. At the time, though, AJ had to train as if he were going to fight a champion as no one really knew just how good (or bad) Charles Martin actually was. More of that bout and Anthony's epic battle with Dillian Whyte in two later, separate chapters.

For now, let's head to the O2 Arena in September, 2015, and take a look at how AJ fared in what was being termed a 'Battle of Britain' against Gary Cornish.

CHAPTER 7

THE BATTLE OF BRITAIN

'It reminds me of the early Tyson phenomenon.
He knocked out everyone . . .'
– LENNOX LEWIS ON JOSHUA'S EARLY PRO FIGHTS

Anthony had taken his 'boxing roadshow' up to Glasgow when he fought the Argentine Hector Avila in his fifth professional fight at the start of March 2014. But Scotland would come to him nine bouts later, when the powerful Gary Cornish headed to AJ's spiritual home, the O2, for a Commonwealth title encounter. Gary, from Inverness, was a popular fighter as highlighted by the many Scots who made the journey down to London to see him in action. The Joshua fight would be Gary's 22nd as a pro and he had, impressively, won all the previous 21. He arrived in London unbeaten and looked set to pose a serious threat to Anthony; he was a tough guy and his team believed he had a good chance of travelling back up to Scotland with that Commonwealth belt.

Gary was a well-liked lad. Anthony had always had time for him and would even link up with him for a boxing dinner talk months after they fought. The promo blurb for the event showed just how friendly the two men are, stating as it did, 'We are delighted to announce that Scotland's No.1 Heavyweight and the mandatory challenger for the British Heavyweight title, Gary Cornish, will be one of the Top Table guests when Anthony Joshua comes to Scotland on Friday 16th June. The only blemish on Cornish's 25 fight resume was at the hands of Joshua – and with Gary having racked up 3 wins since, and AJ becoming World Champion, it will make for interesting discussions between the two boxers.'

Anthony liked his down-to-earth character and his honesty, and the way Gary always went out of his way to help charity, as indeed did the majority of people involved in the fight game. He was a big lad, heavily tattooed with a bald head and could look ominous to opponents . . . but not AJ, who was bigger and even more ominous!

Cornish called himself 'The Highlander' and liked to fight in shorts that featured the Scottish flag. His patriotism also shone through in a particular tattoo on his chest, which said, 'Alba gu bràth' – a Scottish Gaelic phrase meaning 'Scotland forever'. He also had an image of the Saltire shaved into his head. Like Anthony, he was a talented footballer. But also like Anthony, he knew that boxing was the only sport for him when he first put on the pads and boots. It was like coming home for both of them: they had found where they belonged and boxing would provide them both with a good living.

Gary was 6 foot 7 inches, an inch taller than Anthony, and admitted his pride about where he originated, and his love of the area where he was born and grew up inspired him when he fought. He planned to help children in Inverness get into boxing and help as much as he could. This wanting to give something back to the community was close to Anthony's own heart and again helped explain the respect both boxers had for the other. Gary would explain his motivation to *Highland News*, 'I'm proud of where I've come from and what I've achieved. Hopefully it's just the start. Hopefully it will get a lot of people involved. Boxing is doing really well in Inverness just now and you've got two clubs who are doing great things.'

Again like AJ, he admitted boxing had brought focus to his life and helped steer him in the right direction, 'Boxing helped me focus more on life – it's a discipline and one I wished I started a lot earlier than I did. Maybe it would have helped with my behaviour in school if I did! I've seen people offered a lot of stuff and gone down very different paths. I'm lucky I chose boxing and it definitely shows what can happen if you don't have those options.

'You don't really know what that buzz is like until you get into the ring. While I don't look ahead of the next fight, having that schedule in front of me has made me more focused. I haven't really had any problems adapting to going full-time – I used to fit my training in around my job, so I'm now able to get more rest.'

AJ was also patriotic, enjoyed his life in London, and was proud to be fighting once again in his adopted hometown, so it was easily to see why the pundits were dubbing the bout 'The Battle of Britain'. Both men were massive so it would also very much be a battle of the giants. The vacant Commonwealth heavyweight title was up for grabs and unbeaten IBO Inter-Continental champion Cornish was, at 28, looking to be a tough challenge for Joshua. He was also not fazed by the prospect of taking on Anthony at the O2 as he had already won three bouts by a knockout in the capital. In total, Gary had won 12 of his 21 fights by a knockout and Anthony felt he would need to be at his best if he were to quell the threat Cornish posed.

Certainly Cornish's manager Tommy Gilmour believed his man could trouble AJ and that the visit to London was not just a leisure break away to earn a few quid and then speed back up to Glasgow, where he was now based. Tommy told the *Daily Record*, 'It's a huge fight for Gary. There's no doubt it will be his hardest fight to date – and perhaps it's come around three or four fights earlier than we thought. But it's an incredible opportunity to fight a quality boxer for a major title. The great thing about it is that Gary really fancies it. Joshua has the amateur pedigree but he's had less professional fights than Gary. This is two fighters that perhaps have not been tested to the best of their abilities just yet – but they will test each other.'

Cornish was being touted as Scotland's best heavyweight since Dundee's Ken Shaw fought in the 1940s. Shaw won the Midlands counties heavyweight title at the age of 15, but the title was taken away from him because it was open only to over-17s. The former Morgan Academy pupil went on to work as a draughtsman in the Caledon Shipyard in Dundee and was the Scottish heavyweight boxing champion for six years between 1945 and 1950. Nicknamed the 'Gentle Giant', he boxed around the world, including Sweden, USA and South Africa, and sparred for Freddie Mills and eventually fought him for the British title. Mills, however, gave him a badly-cut lip in the first round and the fight ended then. After managing the Scottish boxing team in the Empire Games in Auckland, New Zealand, in 1950, he decided to emigrate there and died there, in 1997, aged 77.

Shaw fought in 40 pro bouts and 320 rounds. His first was in October 1942, when he defeated Tommy Brown in Dundee's Caird Hall and his final one was a loss to Don Mullett in May 1951, at Wellington Town Hall in New Zealand. That curtain call was no easy ride choice – Ken was fighting Don for the New Zealand heavyweight crown, and only lost on points.

So Gary Cornish had something to live up to if he was going to become a bigger hero than Shaw.

And Gilmour was sure he was up to the task, adding, 'Gary is a top prospect. He's Scotland's best heavyweight hopeful for more than 50 years. He only had nine fights as an amateur but he has learned very quickly in the pro ranks. He's ready to go up another level and this is his big chance. It's a wonderful opportunity and an exciting fight for everyone.'

Arguably Cornish's best performance in that 'very quick learning' at pro level came when he won his first big pro crown in July 2013. He would be up against England's Paul Butlin for the International Masters heavyweight championship in Inverness. His manager Gilmour had predicted he would win, telling the press, 'Gary's only been in the ring 23 times in his life but he's undefeated. That tells me he has something. Gary's still a novice but he has the will, and the chin, to succeed.'

And Gary himself was confident he would triumph, telling reporters, 'This will be a difficult fight. It's a great reward for two years of hard work. It will be a chance to show people what improvements I have made since turning pro. I only had nine amateur contests but have been kept busy as a professional as well as having the experience of sparring with some of the top guys like David Price and Dereck Chisora. Butlin has a lot of experience so I will need to be at my best on the night. This is the perfect contest at this point in my career, given the quality of the opponents that Butlin has boxed. I aim to be the champion on 5 July.'

Butlin had gone the distance against Dereck Chisora and was clearly the more experienced of the two boxers. But it was Cornish who won the day, knocking Butlin out in the fifth round with some fine body shots. Butlin was counted out on the canvas. He had won the International Masters crown and was now building up to fights that he and his manager would take him to an even higher level, hopefully with the likes of Anthony Joshua. Boxing fans were already impressed – with how Gary had stepped up a level to take on, and beat, the more experienced and battle-hardy Butlin. One fan commented, 'Cornish won by 5th-round stoppage, scored at 3.08 because Butlin failed to beat the count. Felled by a big left to the body Looked a scoring shot, but very hard to see. Butlin went straight to the deck, rolled around. He was furious as was Carl Greaves in his corner, saying the shot was low. Up till then Cornish was totally dominant. Butlin had little success and was hurt earlier in the fight. I have to say, Cornish looked good, he boxed well, intelligently, a genuinely good performance, Butlin tried but had very little success. Impressive from Cornish, I hope he has a few more at this level – what he lacks in experience and amateur schooling he's making up for in hard work and dedication.'

Another fan added, 'Cornish is a mobile guy for his size and I think he could become a better fighter if he could go full time pro. I mentioned Butlin as a potential fight a while back and was glad to see it made. It was a step up albeit it still at a low level. It's positive for him to get a title and some rounds in a competitive bout because that's what he's been lacking and Butlin is a game fella.

'Not saying Cornish is to go on to become a world class fighter but I don't see why domestic honours would be too far beyond him. He's got some ability and seems relaxed in the ring and hopefully can progress. Just needs to develop better habits in training and skills and could well be challenging for British or Commonwealth title in a year's time.'

While another also saw promise in Gary's win over Butlin, believing it could lead to bigger and better things, 'Saw him fight earlier this year and he looks a solid prospect. He has got the tools to be a half decent heavyweight. His long levers mean he has one hell of a jab if he gets it going. Problem when I saw him was he hurt him early so with like many prospects he forgot the basics and started to load up too much. Butlin was a decent step up for him. A fight every two months against names such as Dorian Darch and Danny Hughes – and by the end of the year he could and should be ready for Commonwealth eliminators.'

Cornish was certainly not afraid of hard work as he prepared for the Joshua fight. In 2012, he had to turn down the chance to spar with Klitshcko at his training camp in Germany because he had a fight to prepare for at the back end of 2012 and the start of 2013. Cornish was booked for fights in December 2012, January 2013 and February 2013. At the time his trainer Laurie Redfern, 65, told BBC Scotland Sport, 'He fought in December, he boxed in January and he's boxing again in February. But Gary loves training. He loves being pushed. He is a very good runner, which is unusual because heavyweights tend to be lazy big guys because they are carrying all that weight. The potential is there. It's just getting it out. If we get him to the 20-fight mark we could hopefully go for a British or Commonwealth title. David Price might move on to the European title next and give up his British or Commonwealth title. It would be great if we could get Gary in a position to go for one of those.'

And Cornish, who was still holding down a full-time job, said his plan was to fight as many as 10 bouts in 2013, 'I've got another fight in three weeks' time. I just want to keep busy and learn. We are just a work in progress at the moment. The knockouts will come later on. We are just trying to build up just now.'

After all the hope and hype, the bell finally sounded for the first round and, unfortunately, for Cornish it proved disastrous. He had grafted for his big chance, working his way up through the bouts, training like a demon and inching ever closer to a title bout. But on 15 July 2015 the gulf in class between himself and the best British boxer for years proved simply too wide to bridge. There was no disgrace in the defeat – as Anthony's record of summarily punching the lights out of previous opponents proved. The man was lightning fast and too hot to handle. His punches were like being hit by a hammer, some rivals had said, and Gary Cornish was simply the latest to learn that. Cornish was brave and determined and his win over Butlin had suggested he might indeed be ready to face someone like AJ when the chance arose.

For the first 30 seconds of the bout Cornish was excellent,

taking the fight to Anthony and landing some fine punches. In his trademark Scotland shorts he looked more than at home in such exalted company. But Joshua, in black shorts, was taking his time, carefully examining his rival, seeing what he had to offer and working his way into the fight. On 60 seconds he unleashed a powerful right and Cornish hit the canvas. The crowd ringside erupted from their seats, but it wasn't quite the end.

Cornish bravely got to his feet and again made an admirable attempt to fight back, only to be caught by a lightning left hook. He came forwards again but a flurry of shots left him dizzy and he tried to cling on to Anthony. But the Londoner was having none of it and a clinical left signalled the end of the Scotsman's dream. He was on the canvas looking dazed and stunned by the outcome: his face puzzled, this was not what he expected but now he knew from grim personal experience the power and pain that Anthony Joshua had in those fists.

Cornish tried to beat the count but was staggering around the ring in despair: it was all over after just 97 seconds. Anthony bowed and saluted the crowd in all four corners and then went to commiserate with the Scotsman. Cornish would return to Glasgow safe in the knowledge he had done his level best to live with the Londoner and would continue his career, always willing to learn and improve. But it would be at a much different, lower level than the one now being mapped out for Anthony.

Still, AJ was honest enough to admit that the big Scot had caused him initial problems and that he was relieved to have got the job done and dusted in super-quick time. As he said, Cornish had the ability to cause problems for plenty of other boxers, as he indeed would do when he reignited his career after this defeat. He told Sky Sports afterwards, 'There's no extra time. Credit to Gary where credit is due. He's a big man and had a solid jab. He came out right away and caught me with a good jab. I could see in his eyes he was thinking, "I've nothing to lose." That made Cornish dangerous. I managed to catch him flush to put him away. It's a 12-round fight and I wasn't trying to dish it all out in round one, but I managed to find shots to get the job done. I was trying to slip his long solid jabs and counter him and he went tumbling down. If I leave it and start taking my time, then it could be me on the end of those shots in five rounds time.

'This is what you do it for. When I'm locked away, I lead a simple life in the gym, playing PlayStation and riding my motorbikes. Then I get to come out and give a display.'

For his part, Cornish said he would take a little downtime and then come back all the stronger for this punishing experience. He said, 'I felt like I let people down because I genuinely believed I could win. It wasn't about the money. It was the chance to become the first Scottish heavyweight to win the Commonwealth title. It wasn't to be but I'll go away and think about what happens next.'

AJ's promoter Eddie Hearn was, once again, beaming like the cat that had got the proverbial cream. He purred, 'We are looking at perfection here. There's not a heavyweight around who can last more than two rounds with AJ.'

But Anthony's bitterest rival Dillian Whyte did not agree with that assessment. He was ringside for the Cornish fight with an eye to his British title fight with Anthony that loomed a couple of months later. Whyte, of course, had beat Anthony in their amateur days and was already predicting he would do the same at pro level when they too met in the O2 Arena.

Whyte had been added to the undercard of the Joshua/ Cornish bout and, after beating Brian Minto for the vacant WBC International Silver Heavyweight Championship, watched AJ in action. Whyte saw off Minto in three rounds and then claimed he would do the same to Joshua, telling the press, 'It wasn't the cleanest, but I did get the job done against Minto. My trainer said that the second round was terrible but he knew I was carrying a heavy shoulder injury. I'll show up in December, don't worry about that. If it was on one arm or one leg, I'll show up in December. I know the Joshua fight is going to be a good, hard fight but I don't want to fight guys with a losing record, when they're mentally already beaten. I'm in the game to put on good fights, test myself and reward the fans.'

But Anthony dismissed Dillian's taunts, saying that unlike his rival, the be-all and end-all of his hopes and dreams did not surround one man. He said, 'My ambition doesn't end with Dillian Whyte. It seems like his ends with me but I am looking to go through him towards a world title. Commonwealth, British, European and then world. Boom, boom, boom. That's the dream for me.'

Anthony Joshua was now a young man with a mission: knock out Whyte and power on towards a world title fight. He sounded confident, powerful and determined to achieve his dream. But would the fight with Dillian Whyte throw him off course? Would he be able to control his emotions and not get involved in a street brawl with a fighter whom he admitted he disliked immensely and whom had beaten him at amateur level. Would he be able to maintain discipline and composure as he tried to even up the score by gaining revenge on Whyte, who seemed intent on winding him up at every juncture?

Or would Whyte triumph again, halting the Joshua juggernaut and putting in jeopardy all those dreams of title fights and world domination? Could one local skirmish be so damaging if AJ lost his head and went toe-to-toe with Whyte? We were about to find out the answers to all these questions as the two boxers headed to a packed O2 Arena 13 days before the Christmas of 2015.

CHAPTER 8

THE GRUDGE MATCH

It's a fact of life in the tough world of heavyweight boxing that every fighter will have an opponent he holds a grudge against. A rival whom, throughout his career, he will box more than once and whom he would probably take on bare-knuckled in a street brawl should the opportunity arise. With the greatest, Muhammad Ali, it was the grizzled battler Joe Frazier who always had the ability to rile him. Their rivalry led to three battles royal, and permanent physical damage to both men. It is also said to have contributed to the Parkinson's that would ultimately hit Ali. Smokin' Joe and Ali battered each other mercilessly during the trio of fights, with two taking place in Madison Square Garden and the third in the Philippines, the so-called 'Thrilla In Manila'. Ali would win two of the fights but at the end of the final bout he collapsed in the ring exhausted, and later admitted, 'it was the closest thing to death'. Theirs was a battle of mind and spirit, as well as physical strength. Joe had been taunted by Muhammad, who called him among other unacceptable things, 'a gorilla', 'ugly' and 'stupid', so it was hardly surprising that he worked himself to a physical peak for that third and deciding contest in Manila.

It was claimed that Ali apologised to Frazier and said that the taunts were not meant; that they were merely to sell the fights and provoke interest, and that they hugged and made up during an All-Star NBA game. But I don't know if Frazier ever forgave Muhammad for his slanders. Before he died, Joe told the Associated Press he felt compassion for the Parkinson's Ali suffered but also commented that Ali had blasphemed by saying, 'I am the greatest!' He said, 'God judges' and added that it was also wrong that Ali had changed his name from Cassius Clay.

For another of Anthony Joshua's boxing heroes, 'Iron' Mike Tyson, the grudge involved Evander 'The Real Deal' Holyfield, whose style of boxing AJ also admired, and hoped to emulate. Tyson lost both battles, much to his anger, and infamously bit off a piece of Holyfield's ear in the second bout in June 1997. It led to Mike being disqualified and losing his boxing licence, although it would eventually be reinstated.

Thankfully, the duo would later become friends and Tyson would even induct Holyfield into the Nevada Boxing Hall of Fame in 2014. The two former boxers had patched up their differences and the Hall of Fame get-together showed them smiling and hugging. Rich Marotta, the president of the Nevada Boxing Hall of Fame, summed up the transformation, telling the *Los Angeles Times*, 'This is the kind of thing we showed is possible in boxing last year at our inaugural induction ceremony – former and even current rivals coming together under the same roof to celebrate boxing. Everyone checks those rivalries at the door. Tyson presenting Holyfield is sheer magic.'

Back in Britain, there was arguably a level of hatred a step or two up from the Tyson/Holyfield encounters – and on a par with the Ali/Frazier run-ins. Yes, step up to the stage Chris Eubank and Nigel Benn. The duo had a deep-seated dislike of each other, essentially because like Ali and Frazier they were chalk 'n' cheese in terms of lifestyle and character. Eubank liked to play the slightly eccentric gent out of the ring, sometimes walking around with a monocle in his eye and wearing smart, 'gentrified' outfits. Benn, on the other hand, was an ex-squaddie, down-to-earth and a 'what you see is what you get' figure. Given the disparities, it was no surprise that the duo hated each other's guts, with Benn taking offence at Eubank's lisp-induced barbs at his lack of style and adjudged coarseness. It led to two big fights, the first of which Eubank won by a knockout in 1990 and a draw three years later. Like Ali and Frazier, and Holyfield and Tyson, the pair would thankfully make their peace in later life and even share a stage for after-dinner events.

And so to Anthony Joshua himself, and his own personal grudge rival. Any fan of AJ will tell you straight away that the one boxer he cannot abide is Dillian Whyte – and that the feeling is mutual. As we have already noted, the duo fought as amateurs, with AJ suffering one of only three losses to his name on the circuit. They would meet again as pros – more of that later in this chapter – and that battle would again leave a sour taste in both of their mouths. And even after seeing off Klitschko in their Wembley megafight – and with the whole world literally in his hands – Anthony, according to the usually reliable *Times* newspaper, would ask his promoter to set up a third battle with Whyte. Ron Lewis, of *The Times*, broke the extraordinary news in May 2017, revealing, 'Anthony Joshua has asked for a rematch with Dillian Whyte, although he is unlikely to face his old rival before next year at the earliest. With a future clash against Tyson Fury depending on the result of a UK Anti-Doping hearing, Joshua, the IBF and WBA heavyweight champion, is understood to have named Whyte when asked by Eddie Hearn, his promoter, who his ideal opponent would be.'

One fan summed up the general feeling of shock – and a belief that Anthony should forget about grudges against a man he had left behind, and a possible street brawl of an encounter, and concentrate on consolidating his position as World No 1, while improving his fighting techniques. The fan commented, 'Joshua should avoid "grudge" matches unless the opponent brings a world title with him. Why would he face Whyte again otherwise unless he becomes a mandatory challenger?' It was a fair comment: a slugfest would hardly prove beneficial to any tweaks in performance Anthony was looking to address as he improved and developed further as a fine boxer, and it suggested a somewhat warped sense of ambition and direction when a calm and collected vision was what was really needed to map out his future. A future that was already exciting enough without taking an unnecessary tangent into brawl territory for ego satisfaction. Anthony had come a long way and had no need to get one over on Whyte, however much he might enjoy doing so.

To understand how his mind was working when he apparently asked his promoter to set up another clash with Dillian, we need to backtrack, first to that amateur fight and then on to the professional bout that would follow some years subsequently. The pair first fought as amateurs in 2009. It was Whyte's first amateur bout and he beat Anthony on points over three rounds, flooring him in the process. Whyte, who was fighting for his local club Chadwell St Mary, had no idea who Anthony was, just that he had notched a couple of knockouts for his Finchley club.

Whyte had previously been a professional kickboxer and admitted he got into boxing only to enhance his skills as a kickboxer, 'I initially got involved with boxing to improve my hand skills for my Muay Thai bouts.' He pointed out that both Klitschko brothers had trained in kickboxing and that it had helped them develop as boxers. Whyte, who was born in Jamaica, where he said he had 'no schooling', moved to the UK when he was 12. In common with Anthony, he felt sport not only changed his life, but saved him. He said, 'I didn't do too well at school, to be honest, but boxing saved me and changed my life. And it was going well, because I knew it was my best chance in life.' Given that they had similar experiences as youths and in boxing, you would imagine they would bond rather than rub each other up the wrong way: not so. The opposite, in fact.

Whyte only had a limited career as an amateur because of a dispute with the Amateur Boxing Association (ABA) over his previous kickboxing work, which led him to turn professional, with a first pro fight in 2011. He now had his first resentment with Anthony as he felt his rival's backroom team had played a part in getting him suspended by complaining loudly that their boy had been in with a pro (when they learned of Whyte's kickboxing career).

Then, in Dillian's ninth fight as a pro, he would find another stick with which to beat Anthony after suffering another suspension from boxing. He beat up Bulgaria's Sandor Balogh in Kent but subsequently failed a drugs test for banned substances. That led to an enforced absence from the ring and would lead to Dillian claiming that Anthony had called him a 'a drugs cheat', a charge Dillian denies to this day.

Whyte was banned from the sport for two years after his appeal against the ban was turned down. He had tested positive for the stimulant methylhexaneamine (MHA), an ingredient in a nutritional supplement called Jack3D. The appeal panel accepted his claim that he did not knowingly take MHA but rejected his appeal because, they argued, he did not do enough to check the supplement's ingredients. 'The supplement was described on the container as "an ultra-intense muscle supplement, giving strength, energy, power and endurance",' Charles Flint QC, the chairman of the appeal tribunal, explained in his written verdict. 'It was plainly intended to be a performance-enhancing supplement which an athlete should only take after having taken great care to ensure that it does not contain a prohibited substance. The athlete took no steps to make any proper enquiries of his manager or coach, any person with medical or anti-doping expertise, or the sports authorities, as to whether the supplement was safe to take. A one-minute search on the internet in respect of Jack3D or (listed ingredient) dimethylamylamine would have revealed that the product might contain a prohibited substance.'

Nicola Newman, UK Anti-Doping Director of Communications and Education, summed up the finding, 'In August 2012,

Down you go . . . Joshua hammers Ukrainian legend Wladimir Klitschko with a powerful right-hander at Wembley, 29 April 2017.

(© AP/REX/Shutterstock)

Left: Cuban reel… Anthony hits powerful Cuban amateur boxer Erislandy Savon with a massive left-hander in a 2012 Olympics bout that tested the Londoner to the limit.

(© Getty Images Sport)

Right: The Italian stallion … Italy's Roberto Cammarelle digs in but cannot halt the advance of Joshua in their gold medal bout at the 2012 Olympics in London.

(© Ivan Sekretarev/AP/REX/Shutterstock)

Left: Fist class … AJ raises his fist in triumph after turning the bout around in the third round of his gold-medal final against a dejected-looking Roberto Cammarelle.

(© Damien Meyer/Getty Images)

Right: I've done it … AJ celebrates during the awards ceremony after lifting the gold medal at London 2012.

(© Jack Guez/Getty Images)

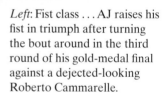

Left: Right track ... AJ powers in with a massive right hand on his way to destroying Eric Molina, the final hurdle before the fight with Klitschko could be officially confirmed.

(© James Crombie/INPHO/REX/Shutterstock)

Right: Wince Martin ... 'Prince' Charles Martin feels the stress as AJ connects with a massive left hand on the way to a second-round win in their fight at London's O2 Arena.

(© Ben Queenborough/BPI/REX/Shutterstock)

Left: Scotland the Brave ... but even the plucky attitude of Gary Cornish could not save him from a second-round defeat at the hands of Joshua at the O2 in London in September, 2015.

(© Leigh Dawney/Getty Images)

Right: Pride and the boy ... Anthony with the MBE he received from Prince Charles in a special ceremony for Britain's Olympic heroes at Buckingham Palace in February 2013.

(© WPA Pool/Getty Images)

Above: 'Take that, pal' . . . Anthony Joshua catches Wladimir Klitschko with an uppercut that leaves the Ukrainian reeling during their Wembley fight in front of 90,000 fans, 29 April 2017. *(© Richard Heathcote/Getty Images)*

Below: The famous five . . . Anthony grabs hold of his promoter Eddie Hearn while three other members of his team proudly hold his title belts after his eleventh-round KO of Wladimir Klitschko in April 2017.

(© Richard Heathcote/Getty Images)

the Medicines and Healthcare products Regulatory Agency ruled that products containing methylhexaneamine needed to be removed from the UK market. The fact that Mr Whyte purchased a product containing this ingredient after that date should remind all athletes that they need to be vigilant when considering supplementing their diet.'

Whyte's lawyer called the judgment 'harsh' and 'unfair' and it seemed to me that the boxer had received a tough deal. In July 2012 Welsh boxer Enzo Maccarinelli had been banned for six months after failing a random drugs test, when he also tested positive for MHA. The former WBO world cruiserweight champion admitted he had taken a product from a combat magazine but said he was not aware of its ingredients.

Like Whyte, he also blamed the abuse on naivety and ignorance, stating, 'Following my fight against Shane McPhilbin in March, I was extremely surprised and disturbed to have tested positive for a banned substance known as methylhexaneamine. I purchased a product called Dexaprine that contained this banned substance from a combat magazine. The advert stated that it was an approved substance and I checked the ingredients which had no reference to any banned substance that I was aware of. In fact, it also stated that it was suitable for athletes.

'I have since found out that this "fat burner" contained a substance and consequently I failed a dope test, albeit with a very low reading. I wish to state that this substance was in no way used to gain any advantage in the ring or enhance my performance and whilst I appreciate that it may look that way, I would certainly never cheat or cut corners in my preparation. I have been tested over 20 times in my career and have never failed any random or post-fight doping test, but on this occasion, due to my naivety, I have tested positive for a banned substance.'

Of course no abuse of banned substances can be condoned or excused, even if ignorance be the reason behind it. It is the duty of every responsible professional athlete, not to mention their manager or coach, to look after their body and enforce rigorous checks on any supplements they may be considering. But there was certainly a discrepancy in a six-month ban for Maccarinelli and the two-year one for Dillian Whyte. Dillian himself would later tell BBC Sport that he felt he had been made an example of. 'I was totally up front with them and I didn't get any credit for it. If I were taking steroids and I lied to them I would probably have been better off because there seems to be people in boxing taking steroids, lying about it and getting less than me. I don't know why they would make an example of me.'

The problem for Whyte now was that he could not appeal again – it was a case of one appeal and one only. Dillian was forced on the sidelines for a couple of years. And all the while he could see his nemesis, Anthony Joshua, scale ever greater peaks. While training for his last pro fights before the ban, he had watched Anthony claim gold at London 2012 and now he would have to watch from afar as the Finchley boy took the pro world by storm, winning his first nine fights before Whyte's comeback. Dillian finally returned to action on 21 November 2014. Yet just days earlier he had shown that his simmering resentment against AJ had not disappeared. No, he was still angry and wanted revenge ASAP, as he told Buncey's Boxing Podcast on ESPN, 'He's so insecure and so jumpy about losing to me. When anyone tries to ask him about it, he says, "It was 10 years ago, I was only beaten by one point." I say, "Listen, we fought at the end of 2009 and we haven't been boxing for 10 years, so that doesn't make sense. We've only been boxing for five or six years! It wasn't 10 years ago, and I didn't win by one point. I won unanimously and I knocked him down.

'We fought a while ago and as far as I was concerned that was it. Even when he was in the Olympics, I was supporting him, saying there was no way he could lose. But then a couple of months ago he ripped some stuff about me to the press. He later said he didn't mean it and that they'd misinterpreted him, but it p***** me off to be honest.'

Whyte claimed that he had confronted AJ when they both took part in Wladimir Klitschko's Austrian training camps. He said, 'We were out in Austria at a training camp and I pulled him up on it. I said to him, "Listen, we definitely have to fight again because I don't like what you said and, where I come from, people can't say things like that about other people. We're professionals so let's settle it in the ring.' He's gone on and done well so far as a pro, so I just leave him to it. I just hope we do get to fight because I think it's a good fight for Britain.'

Sure, it would be a good fight for the fans and for the TV companies who could cash in on the heated rivalry. But was it a good fight for Anthony Joshua as he continued to push forwards on an upward trajectory? I did not have the feeling it was; it had the makings of a fight that would only end with him getting involved in another scrap, and there would no doubt be many unsavoury comments from Whyte, and Anthony could be tempted to reply. OK, it did provide the opportunity to avenge a defeat, but in my eyes the bout benefitted Dillian much more than it did Anthony. The latter had everything to lose and only sated pride and ego to gain.

But in the end, money talked, as did Anthony's absolute insistence that the fight should take place. It was scheduled for 12 December 2015, at London's O2 Arena in Docklands. The duo would do battle for the vacant British heavyweight title. The bout was revealed on 14 September, which meant there would be three months for jibes and insults to be traded – and many were. Indeed, the barbs began four days before the announcement, when Anthony and Dillian came face to face at AJ's press conference for his imminent bout against Gary Cornish for the vacant Commonwealth heavyweight crown. Whyte was on the undercard to take on Brian Minto, and seemed to relish the opportunity to have a dig at Anthony during the joint press conference between Whyte and Minto and AJ and Cornish. The four men sat together on a long table in front of the media and things quickly got out of hand as Whyte focused on riling Anthony rather than his imminent opponent, Minto.

Anthony played his part, too, after hinting that Dillian would be his next opponent if both men got past their respective opponents on this card. He riled Whyte by saying he would 'soon have his five minutes of fame', a clear hint that they would fight soon. Whyte replied, 'Stop being fake, be yourself. This is not you. Stop fooling the people.'

Anthony said, 'In what sense?'

Whyte then answered, 'Punk. Be yourself. I am going to hurt you. Little punk. You are a fool. You are going to get bashed up.'

To which Anthony said, 'You are lucky to be on my undercard.' Which ended with Whyte calling him a 'scumbag' and saying, 'Don't talk rubbish.'

Dillian was so fired up he continued his tirade after filming for Sky Sports stopped. First up, he got in a jibe to answer the time Anthony allegedly called him a 'drugs cheat'. Now Whyte turned the tables on Anthony over his own drug offences years earlier. Whyte quipped, 'He is a drug dealer from Watford. He has probably changed a bit, grown up, been media trained, had a sports psychologist. He has achieved a lot, won a gold medal, but he just needs to be himself. He is a robot and I can't wait for those batteries to run out so I can see what will happen.

'I have done it the hard way, grinding. Eddie [Hearn, Anthony's promoter] has done a great job handpicking these guys for him at the right time. He is a good prospect but I don't like him as a person. I think he is a very scummy person who tries to belittle people and speak a certain way. Then he acts a certain way. How am I lucky to be on his undercard? I am on it because I whupped his a**e. He is silly, a silly boy.'

Therein lay another big resentment for Dillian: the belief that while he had been forced to fight for scraps in boxing because of his ban, Anthony had been a beneficiary of the silver-spoon treatment. In Whyte's eyes, Anthony had been pumped up as the next big thing, earning thousands on Sky TV against 'bums', all the while he was having to fight every step of the way to make his name, earning a mere pittance compared to AJ's wages. That resentment, plus the ones over the drugs ban and the constant ping-ponging of verbal jibes, had propelled Whyte into a frenzy of hatred. One that could only be sated by a battle in the ring and, as he saw it, inflicting a second defeat on Anthony.

The fight clearly would not be an easy one for Anthony. He was facing a man who would dearly love to win and a fighter who was undefeated in 16 professional contests, with 13 knockouts. Whyte had also made an extremely smart move with his back-up team – he was now in the hands of Wladimir Klitschko's trainer Johnathon Banks. Whyte said, 'Johnathon Banks is a very important part of my game now. It's all about technique, being faster, being more accurate. I'm completely different to everyone Anthony Joshua has fought. Dillian Whyte will be victorious. I'll go for the win whichever way I can get it but I definitely want to knock him out.'

The verbal assaults from both sides continued right up to the night of the grudge match itself. In fact, Sky compiled a list of the very best ones, from a variety of press conferences, that showed just how worked up both men had become by 12 December. It made interesting, sometimes amusing, reading as they tried to outdo each other and was, of course, a real boon to Sky as they tried to drum up massive interest for the fight, which would be shown on their Box Office channel. The list of insults read as follows:

WHYTE: 'I'm the predator that smiles just before the kill. I know blood is coming. I can taste it even before it starts running so my juices are flowing. I'm licking my lips.'
JOSHUA: 'I went on to do good things as an amateur and as I turned pro people said, "Dillian is coming for you". Come on now, I'm not worried about anyone.'

WHYTE: 'I expect him to be psyched up, coming out raging and trying to destroy me because he's got the world to lose. He's money-orientated so he knows that if he loses here, the big pay-days are going to stop for a while.'

JOSHUA: 'Since turning pro, I said, "Dillian can't be mentioned in the same sentence as me." He bit at that comment. He used that as a way to fuel his popularity and build himself up which is how he's got our fight.'

WHYTE: 'I don't know, he must have been drunk or something, he called me a drug cheat and said he couldn't take me serious and I only won [against him] because I had a kickboxing fight before. It got a bit heated and I offered him out to fight me and then it got calmed down.'

JOSHUA: 'You're lucky to be on my undercard!'

WHYTE: 'I've humbled him in the ring before and I'll humble him again. I remember his friends were giving it before the fight last time and I said I would knock him out. I almost knocked him out.'

JOSHUA: 'He beat me years ago. Many years ago. He seems to be bringing that into the future with him. I'm cool. If you think you can still beat me and that I'm that same kid, let's get it on at The O2 on December 12. We'll go to war.'

WHYTE: 'If people say Anthony Joshua is a bad man with a ruthless side to him, I am saying he is no bad man. He is a good boy. He is a good boxer but he is a good boy.'

JOSHUA: 'He's running his mouth as per usual. I'm out on the streets running and getting in my cardio – that's all I'm doing. We're going to clash.'

WHYTE: 'That's not a real man. He's not real, he's like a

housewife that is being controlled. What he's doing isn't natural. He's sitting there like a robot. I cannot wait for his batteries to run out.'

JOSHUA: 'I asked Dillian to explain what he means [by calling me a fake] and he can't answer. I did ask him what he means because I don't understand myself. I just don't have a clue. I just do my thing.'

Despite the constant barbs, both men were taking the prospect of the actual fight deadly seriously. Quite right, too. Boxing is a dangerous sport and one miscalculation or insufficient preparation can end in major injury, or even tragedy. It was one thing to have the final say with insults in front of the press conference cameras, but quite another to have victory in the ring, where it really mattered. Anthony understood that and soon got down to the serious business of sorting out his training camp and how he would approach the fight. The bout had been scheduled and now it was time to work hard for a successful outcome. Anthony returned to basics for the fight; to what he knew best, to what he knew worked and where it worked. He returned to Sheffield, to the GB training centre for its future Olympics stars. A refuge away from the hype and the hassle and the constant niggling from Whyte. He locked himself away with his trainer, Rob McCracken, sparring for hours, running the necessary miles and putting in the heavy lifts with the weights.

It was hard work but it would surely be worth it: he was a much more talented boxer than Whyte but his rival had the brute strength that could conceivably deliver a knockout punch if Anthony dropped his guard, even for a moment. McCracken stressed to his boy the importance of concentration, total concentration and the perils awaiting him if he dropped his hands for even a few seconds. That had been an area the duo worked on tirelessly, and would continue to do over the years. If Anthony had one weakness, it was that he could lower his hands and invite an opponent on. Someone once said to me that he did it deliberately – that he sometimes got a little bored and wanted to add some edge, some danger, to proceedings! If so, it was a move covered in dynamite, and an explosion that could end up in Anthony's head. Anthony also spent time at the Matchroom gym in Essex and, as always, ensured he got enough rest, enough sleep and exactly the right combination of meals and snacks as he went about his work.

A couple of days before the fight, Anthony and Dillian had to head back to London for a final pre-fight press conference. In comparison to previous ones, it was almost civil! And Anthony surprised many people by using it to reveal that, as he looked back on it right now, he could see the positives of that amateur defeat at the hands of his rival. He explained that it had given him 'a kick up the backside' and given him many clues as to what he needed to do to become a better fighter, and how to become a fighter who would win and keep on winning. He said, "My first two fights had been knockouts and when I first started boxing I thought I was the man. But then I fought Dillian, who was very experienced. He had the ring generalship of a kick-boxer. We fought, he knocked me down, but my heart had the courage to pick myself up and fight on until the final bell. It gave me the realisation that I had to step up my game.

'I was a raw novice. I had only trained for six months. I was on a tag [because of an offence] at the time so couldn't even train full time, I had to leave the gym early at 7.30pm to be back for 8pm. OK, I made some mistakes, but I had the courage to get up and fight on. So I added some arsenal to my game, and built myself up, and that's why I am here now.'

His words were measured and showed a degree of class and thought after the hyperbole and nastiness both he and Dillian had engaged in during previous tête-à-têtes with Fleet Street's finest. It made me admire this boy from nowhere all the more and I absolutely expected him to now go into that ring and claim victory. He seemed at ease with himself and with his condition and the fight generally. He could probably have got into the ring right then and whipped his rival – certainly if Whyte's continued hot-headedness was anything to go by.

Dillian continued his bad mouthing to the bitter end, telling reporters, 'I can't wait to smash this robot to pieces. I grew up around big brothers and most big guys crumble under pressure. He's made a mistake taking this fight. I'm not old, I've got ambition. I'm undefeated. I believe I can be a world champion and I am going to do what I do naturally, which is to fight.'

Finally, the time for talk was over, and the Finchley flyer and the Brixton brawler stood across from each other in the ring in London's O2 Arena. The moment of truth had arrived for both men. Defeat for Whyte would be less catastrophic than for Anthony, who had considerably more to lose, such as potential championship bouts with the likes of Klitschko and a mapped-out road to superstardom and international fame and acclaim. But he was still a tough cookie and would not collapse at the first heavy punch. His pride would carry him through the battle – he still believed Anthony had slighted him over the years and that it should be him, not AJ, who should be the golden boy. And now he finally had the chance to prove it, under the lights of the O2, and with the boxing world watching.

But Anthony was also inspired by a need to correct that loss many years previously in the amateur ranks, so motivation in terms of revenge remained on both sides. You could tell it by the way they stared each other out as the ref brought them together before the bell. This was a grudge match and both were hellbent on destroying the other. Anthony had predicted he would win in three or four rounds but it would last longer and would leave both men knowing they had been in a battle.

The two men arrived in their own unique way. Anthony, as was his want, walked to the ring with the sound of rap music blaring out and massive cheers. Whyte arrived after him, but to the sound of jeers as well as cheers. It was clear from the very start who the majority had come to support.

Round one saw them psyching each other out and both landing exploratory jabs. Neither wanted to be counted out within three minutes: neither of their egos could have lived with that humiliation. But Anthony suddenly threw caution to the wind and caught Dillian with two powerful left hooks, already bringing the crowd to their feet in anticipation of a swift KO. When the bell went, AJ seemed to connect with Whyte after it had sounded and that caused temporary pandemonium as Whyte hit back and the ref had to intercede. Back-up teams from both sides also jumped into the ring to help separate the fighters, although their intervention could have itself caused problems. Sense finally prevailed, the ring emptied and the boxers sat down in their respective corners. This was clearly going to be a night where rules would be tested and the ref's patience tried to the limit.

The ref sensibly spoke to both boxers at the start of Round 2, telling them to calm down and stick to the rules. Anthony landed a powerful uppercut but Dillian then hit back with a series of masterful shots, stunning Anthony and sending him reeling. The turnaround in fortunes was a surprise, unexpected as it had appeared AJ had the upper hand at the end of the previous round. Now it was he who was hanging on at the bell. Was this going to be a feature of Anthony's biggest fights – that initial blood rush and the brink of knocking an opponent out, only to then seem worn out by those efforts and letting his guard down? It is worth mentioning as 16 months later, he would virtually repeat the sequence against Klitschko, initially battering the Ukrainian, then letting him back in as he hung back to draw breath, before a third period where he would appear revitalised and refreshed, and knock him out.

But if it were to repeat throughout his career, there feasibly could come a time when Anthony might be caught out and knocked out. Where he might be punished heavily during the period when he tried to get his breath back. No doubt that would be something his team would be working on as his career progressed and as he put more rounds behind him. It could have been down to the fact that he was in the habit of knocking rivals out within two rounds, and had been so intent on an early knockout that he temporarily took the stuffing out of himself, so that he needed to stay on the ropes for a few minutes to recharge his batteries. Rob McCracken and his team would analyse each performance and point out the pitfalls of trying to blast opponents out of the ring early on, but when a boxer is hellbent on destroying an opponent all logic could go out the window. And AJ certainly wanted to knock down Dillian (and later Wladimir) in a hurry, but nearly paid a heavy price in that bruising Round 2 against Whyte.

Round 3 was more measured, with both men making inroads but no clear winner. But it was worth noting at the bell that Anthony had now gone three rounds, one more than the other bouts in his burgeoning pro career! In Round 4 Anthony took the initiative and had Dillian on the defensive. His right-hand hammer blows were surely leaving a mark on Whyte, who appeared happy enough to soak up the punishment and take the bout well beyond Anthony's comfort zone. This was certainly new territory for the Finchley bomber: could he cope with the fight going towards the halfway mark?

Round 5 saw AJ consolidate his position as the man in charge. The early tiredness had gone and he was landing big punches and those devastating upper cuts that were rapidly becoming his trademark. Whyte, to his credit, soaked them up but the damage was being done and he was clearly tiring as the bell went. Whyte's bravery was summed up as he took one massive right hand to the head, stumbled slightly, but refused to go down. Whyte was proving that he was more than worthy to be in this big title fight; he may have trash talked during the build-up but he was walking the walk with this gritty, admirable showing at the O2.

Round 6 and Anthony seems content to keep up his attack, all the while ensuring Whyte does not sneak any punches in.

His boxing is measured now, he knows he is in control of the evening and his confidence is high. He has gone six rounds and looks fit and menacing, and full of energy. His training is paying off, as is the fact that he is bigger and stronger than his rival. The highlight of the round is when the men exchange powerful right hands to the head, and each smiles as if to compliment the other on the artistry of the respective shots.

The bell went for Round 7, and we were nearing the end of the road for Dillian Whyte, who had proved himself a brave opponent with a big heart. Whyte hit AJ with two opening shots but was then caught by a big right as he tired, his defences falling. He staggered across the ring and Anthony moved in for the kill like a hawk tuning in on its unfortunate prey. A massive uppercut that Dillian was powerless to thwart, and he was on the ropes . . . literally. He had one hand holding the ropes and the ref pushed Anthony away and rushed over to remove Dillian's gum shield. The war was over: revenge was complete. Anthony raised his right arm in triumph. Mission accomplished; time to celebrate and move on. But he knew he had been in a fight and that the man who once beat him as an amateur had given everything. Anthony Joshua had come of age, but so had Dillian Whyte. There would be room for both men in the heavyweight division although it would be Anthony who would continue on his rise to superstardom, the biggest fights and the biggest paychecks.

AJ was the new British heavyweight champion, he was happy, his team were happy and Sky were happy that their Box Office customers had had their money's worth. Sky Sport bosses knew they had a winner in Anthony and their good judgment in backing him early on in his career was already proving to be a money-spinner, and the takings could now only get bigger as he moved on to bigger bouts.

After the fight Anthony was delighted but not getting carried away. He said, 'Lovely reception – and it turned it into a street fight at the start! Dillian was the perfect fight for this stage of my career. It was a tough fight, I made it tough for myself. That's what I need, the experience, I can look forward, some mistakes I made in there which I can't take to the top level. I am going to keep on building and building and building. I found my way and I found my rhythm. I had the same power in the final round as I had in the opening one. It is not about the rivalry – I knew I had the strength to knock him out. I didn't prove too much but now I have the British title. And big respect to everyone who came out for me. People say can he take a shot? I took a couple of silly ones. I learned stuff about myself that I can take into 2016 and progress.'

Yet even as the plaudits rained down Anthony remained stoical about the chances of becoming world champion any time soon, telling BBC Radio 5 Live, 'A world title fight is still far away. Becoming an elite athlete in such a tough sport, it doesn't happen overnight but I've got the desire, ambition and the team around me to do it but I don't want to rush it because when I get there, I want to stay there.'

That sounded like the Anthony Joshua we were getting to know – measured and reflective, certainly a long way from the rather hot-headed boxer who had gone into the Whyte fight determined to avenge previous slights and that amateur defeat. A boxer who could have blown it all by ending up in a virtual street brawl because his judgment was clouded by thoughts of revenge. Anthony would surprise commentators by eventually admitting that he was not frightened by the prospect of defeat; that he would simply shrug his shoulders and return and recover. He would say, 'Almost every boxer loses at some time. If I take a loss I will do what great fighters have done before – look and learn why it happened, how it happened and make the adjustments.'

That attitude was certainly surprising. I had never heard a world-class boxer voice it and it highlighted how Anthony viewed his job and indeed life. If he had no fear of losing, he had nothing to lose, and that maybe helped explain how he had become such an explosive and refreshingly new talent in the ring. He fought with freedom and was a breath of fresh air in a boxing heavyweight division that had become all too stale and predictable in an era dominated by the Klitschko brothers.

My good friend and top boxing commentator, Pat Sheehan, had predicted that Anthony would become a boxing legend who would rake in the cash and, after the victory over Whyte, revealed that AJ was already around £3million richer. Writing in the *Daily Express*, he said:

> Anthony Joshua has hit the jackpot before he has even fought for the world heavyweight title. The Londoner is understood to have raked in around £3million for the seventh-round destruction of Dillian Whyte at London's O2 earlier this month. Unbeaten Joshua recently signed a five-year deal with promoter Eddie Hearn of Matchroom that included a cut of the pay-per-view sales, and that has led directly to the big numbers many fighters can only dream of.

The 18,000 capacity O2 sold out within six hours for the bout against Whyte and pay-per-view sales have been described as 'staggering'. Joshua, 26, is the most sought-after heavyweight in the division with the Klitschko brothers Wladimir and Vitali trying to persuade him to sign with their company K2 Promotions.

On the other side of the Atlantic, fight guru Al Haymon has been signing up British boxers like James DeGale and Lee Selby but he too lost out on Joshua, who has been with Hearn since he won the gold medal at the London Olympics. In April, Joshua bids to extend his winning run to 16 when he fights again at London's O2 with the opponent yet to be named. Joshua has already said he would welcome a rematch against Whyte who gave him his biggest test to date and came close to causing a shock before he was eventually KO'd.

I couldn't see the logic in a rematch with Whyte – not at this stage, anyway. Anthony had clearly been the more powerful and a rematch would surely end in the same manner. It was not on the road map to the world title; it could be a fight that made more sense way further down the line.

Clearly, promoter Eddie Hearn saw Joshua/Whyte 2 was not on the immediate agenda as he steered Anthony towards fights that would earn him a crack at a world title. Yet by May 2017, when AJ had won his three world crowns, the old familiar calls for another showdown with Whyte rang out. With AJ himself apparently at the forefront of the demands. Old habits die hard – and so, it seems, do grudges. Would Dillian Whyte become Anthony's Holyfield to Tyson, or his Frazier to Ali? If the past reflected the future, very probably…

CHAPTER 9

CHAMPION OF THE WORLD

The boy from Watford would finally reach the top of the boxing mountain in April 2016, when he won the world heavyweight crown. Admittedly, it was the IBF version, but it still counted as a world title, although some punters still argued that you were only a *true* champion if you had lifted the WBA, WBO or WBC crowns, or preferably, all four. Anthony made it clear that he planned to lift the other three *as well as* the IBF, such was the level of his ambition. But it was a case of one mountain peak at a time, and the IBF was the first to be conquered.

Anthony had signed to challenge for the IBF in February 2016, with the fight due a couple of months later. He would take on Charles Martin, the American holder of the crown. AJ had won all 15 of his professional fights so far, all of them knockouts, and this seemed the next logical step in his career. He had discussed it with his manager, his trainer and his promoter and when Eddie Hearn had suggested it was worth a go, AJ had simply shrugged and said, 'Yeah, let's get it on.' He was typically laid back and not in the least worried by the threat Martin might pose. He was confident he could see off the American with the minimum of damage and seal his first world heavyweight title. Of course, he was not complacent, as his efforts in pre-fight training would confirm, but he had always been a confident boy, so why change now, just because the big time loomed?

When the bout was announced, AJ told reporters, 'Fighting for the heavyweight world title has been a dream of mine since I turned professional. I feel privileged to have the opportunity to turn that dream into reality. Martin is a great fighter and a hungry competitor so I am going to have to produce the performance of my career to claim that belt.'

Martin was aged 29 and had won 23 and drawn one of his 24 fights and had beaten Vyacheslav Glazkov for the vacant IBF belt a few months earlier. He talked a damned good fight, even boasting what he would do when the bout was signed, 'I'm coming to the UK to make a statement that I am the best heavyweight in the world and no one is taking my title. I'm world champion, so that doesn't mean just sit back and make easy defences in the US. It means facing the biggest challenges out there.'

But would he be able to back it up in the ring? Anthony felt he was not even going to be as dangerous as Dillian Whyte, telling the press, 'He's not my toughest opponent yet. But, then it might be a different story come April 9. Right now looking at Charles, he's a very good counter puncher. He's laid back. He doesn't work the full round. So, it should be a nice controlled fight. So, I don't think it'll be like the Dillian Whyte fight. That was a tough fight. We work. We're both hungry. The guy was very strong to the head. That was a tough fight for sure. So, I don't think Charles will impose those kind of threats that Dillian did.'

That was a compliment certainly to Whyte, but not as generous to Martin, who AJ clearly did not rate as tough a customer as his arch enemy from Brixton. Indeed, Anthony predicted that he would win the fight in the sixth round, while Whyte was still standing then.

So just how good was Martin, who called himself 'Prince Charles', and how long would he likely last? Top boxing analyst Steve Bunce described him thus in *The Independent* when it was announced he would fight Anthony: 'Martin followed great fighters like Larry Holmes, Riddick Bowe, Evander Holyfield and Lennox Lewis as the IBF champion. He is a nice guy and can fight a bit, but he is the weakest IBF champion ever and it is possible his payday for winning the belt is the lowest ever received by a champion in a title fight.' Steve claimed Martin got $250,000 for the fight that won the belt, while AJ is reported to have earned £3million for his victory over Dillian Whyte. His popularity and fame (or even infamy) was also apparent in that he had just 7,000 Twitter followers as this book went to the printers, while AJ had 1.15 million.

Just from those facts and figures it was clear that Martin was no Lennox Lewis or Evander Holyfield and, probably, not even a Frank Bruno or Joe Bugner in terms of talent, and would not draw the decent crowds they could. His trip to London and the

O2 was a money-spinner for him, not because he was a great champion, but because he was fighting a new British hero who could take the belt, and whom the public were eager to see live.

But what of his fights pre the Joshua battle? Well, he had turned pro in 2012 and beat some fairly reasonable names the following year, including Joey Dawejko and Glendy Hernandez. The Dawejko fight took place in Hollywood, California, and Martin was the first man to stop the Philadelphia flyer. He then beat the tough Cuban Hernandez, who had won all ten of his previous bouts. Martin's punches ended that record in the fourth round of a scheduled six.

In April 2014, Martin landed his first title, the WBO NABO heavyweight crown when he knocked out another unbeaten rising star, Alexander Flores, again with a fourth round hammer blow. Martin would now successfully defend his title in five clashes, three by knockouts and the other pair by a technical knockout. So he appeared to be no mug, or was it that the men put up against him were merely 'bums' as the Americans like to call no-hopers? For our purposes, a bout on April 25, 2015, on the undercard of a Wladimir Klitschko fight, gives us a clearer insight as the man he beat that night was a Brit. Step forward Tom Dallas, a boxer I should make clear right now, is no 'bum', but an honest pro who has worked hard to make his way in the fight game. Tom, from Chatham, Kent, was rated 34th out of 40 in the current rankings of British boxing as this book went to the printers and his 25-fight career read 17 wins, 12 by knockouts, and eight losses.

He lost to Martin in the first round of their battle on the Klitschko v Bryant Jennings undercard, by way of a technical

KO. Kent Online summed up the outcome, saying, 'Tom Dallas' American dream was over inside the first round in New York on Saturday. Chatham heavyweight Dallas, who turned 30 on Thursday, was hoping to celebrate his birthday with a massive upset in the ring against Charles Martin. Fighting at the world-famous Madison Square Garden venue, Dallas was bidding to win the WBO NABO title and inflict a first defeat on Martin. But the fight went the way many expected with Dallas immediately troubled by Martin's longer reach. The fifth professional defeat of Dallas' career came just before the end of the first round when the referee stepped in after a stunning left punch had the Chatham man struggling.'

Before the fight Dallas had said he thought he 'had a chance' and even gave AJ a namecheck, adding, 'I have seen him [Martin] and, yes, he punches hard but so does anyone that's 18 stone. I know you can't compare them but I've sparred with David Price and Anthony Joshua and they hit hard. He is hittable and can be sloppy. I won't be laying down. I am going to put up a fight.'

Fair play to Dallas, he put his heart into it and trained well, but maybe suffered because he had been out of action for the previous 19 months. His last fight previous to the April 2015 bout was back in September 2013 and so ring rust could have played a part.

But the fact that Martin had caught him with such a powerful left shot suggested the American was not to be dismissed as fodder for the Joshua fight. That dangerous left hook was a menace if taken lightly, and had already ended the ambitions of many big men in the division.

'Prince Charlie's' biggest break would come outside the

boxing ring in December 2015 – and it was down to another Brit, the always controversial Tyson Fury. Fury had won the IBF crown with an unexpected victory over Wladimir Klitschko a few weeks earlier. The surprise win ended Klitschko's reign as champion in Düsseldorf, Germany, after Manchester's Fury triumphed on a points verdict. It meant Fury was now WBA, IBF and WBO champion.

But Fury decided he did not want to meet the mandatory IBF challenger, Yacheslav Glazkov. Instead, he would take on Klitschko again, in a rematch. So who would now take on Glazkov for the now vacant IBF title? Step forward Martin, who had been preparing for a fight with Dominic Breazeale but now abandoned plans for that encounter to prepare for a bust-up with Ukrainian Glazkov for a winner-takes-all prize. 'I wanted to fight both fights (Breazeale and then Glazkov at a later date),' Martin would tell the Orange County Register. Eventually, they (my team) made me come to the conclusion that this was obviously a bigger deal and I was like OK. I was in camp for Breazeale for eight-nine weeks, so we took a week off and went back to camp.'

The 'Prince' showed he was no shrinking violet and that he had a big opinion of himself and his talent, by adding, without an hint of irony, 'I'm training to be a superstar. If you train to mediocre, then that's what you will be. You have to work like you want to stay a world champion and train like you want that longevity in the sport and that's what I've been doing.'

The fight that would usher in a new IBF heavyweight king was settled to take place on January 16, 2016, in Brooklyn, New York. Yet, remarkably considering it was for a title, it would not be the main event. The headliner would see fellow American

Deontay Wilder make the third defence of his WBC title against Poland's Artur Szpilka. Deontay was obviously the big beast as far as the States was concerned and would continue to be the man away from these shores who would be the biggest threat to Anthony's supremacy.

Not that Martin was concerned at playing second fiddle. 'I'm feeling really blessed to get this opportunity,' he told reporters in the US at the press conference to announce the fight. 'I want to become a world champion so I can go down in history as a top heavyweight. Glazkov is a great fighter. He's undefeated, so I know it's going to be a tough fight, but I'm coming in to be victorious. I'm getting ready and training hard so I can go out there and get that win.'

Glazkov was equally grateful at the unexpected opportunity. 'I am looking forward to getting back in the ring and finally getting my chance to fight for a world title,' he said. 'I want to thank everyone who helped me get to this place in my career.'

I bet he did – from nowhere, both he and Martin were now in line for a crack at a world title neither could have imagined. Martin claimed the title by stopping his opponent in the third round when Glazkov retired injured. Afterwards, Martin was keen to prove he was no one-hit wonder, saying, 'I want to unify the titles – I want to fight, I have not had a fight tonight. I am sorry for him, it is unfortunate he was unable to finish the fight. It was meant to be. We had 12 rounds and I was pacing myself. I was going to pick it up as I went along. I didn't even get what he was doing. He was scared. You could see it in his eyes. I still wanted to fight. It's 12 rounds, that's what I trained for.'

Martin claimed he decided to take on Anthony next because

he was 'a superstar' and he wasn't interested in going down the easy route, although the reported £5million he would bank probably helped sway his mind towards the bout. The fight would be broadcast by Showtime in America and their pre-bout press conference with both fighters gave an interesting and revealing insight into the psyche of Martin and Anthony. It was then that Martin claimed he was coming over to the UK because he wanted to show he was a great champion by beating a superstar, unlike others who would sidestep the likes of AJ, 'I ain't scared, man. I'm here for a reason. And, you know, over here he's a superstar, man. You know what I'm saying? And we want to take on all these big names. He was the biggest name that we could see this far, you know, besides Tyson Fury. Tyson Fury was already in with Klitschko, and Deontay Wilder was busy. You know what I'm saying?

'All the other big names were taken. You know, I'm saying at the time he was the only one that was open, available. So, we figure why not do that? We want to make a name and make a mark on the sport. You know what I mean? That's what I want to do. You know, I want people to know that he's down for whatever, whenever, however. If I got to come all the way over here to do it, I'm down for whatever. I'm down for whatever, man.'

They were brave words from a boxer unknown in the UK, unknown but who had managed to lift a title via a backdoor route. Martin soon found out the British sporting public were not as fair as had been suggested, and that they would never warm to a foreigner who was taking on their boy. 'It is all entertainment,' Martin laughed as he was roundly booed by members of the public who attended a ring workout at York

Hall in East London. 'Handling the crowd and the people is a good thing, it's entertainment, but when I step in the ring, it's business. It's strictly business because you can get hurt in this ring. You can walk out different to how you walked in, so I will take it seriously. That's why I train 100 per cent for each fight.

'I can't get caught up in that sort of stuff,' he added at the press conference that followed the mini workout. 'I just keep things simple. I don't complicate anything. Getting too focused on other people, I don't have time for that. All I have time for is training and getting ready for this fight.'

You had to admit that Martin was not only up for the fight, but that he talked a good fight before the actual battle in the ring. He seemed confident in his own ability, calm and collected and, if the reality matched the talk, could potentially pose problems for Anthony. He was a world champion and appeared to be a notch up from the likes of Dillian Whyte. In the event, he would prove to be a notch down from Dillian, but his pre-fight belief certainly helped put bums on seats. The British boxing public were intrigued to see if he could deliver, and if AJ could cope with him if he did, or whether it would be yet another hopeful who talked the talk and bit the dust when confronted with the man mountain that Anthony Joshua had now become.

For his part, AJ was confident that he would see off the threat of Martin and felt his experiences against Dillian Whyte would hold him in good stead for the Martin bout. Anthony also put in a ring workout on the same day as Martin and then spoke of how he was convinced that the tough battle with Whyte could only serve to iron the flaws in his boxing, including a tendency to aim to win with one big punch, when more patience was what was really called for, and to show more dexterity with his feet than the Whyte fight. Joshua said of his analysis of the Whyte fight, 'There's some good and a lot of bad. I need to keep my shape. When I'm rolling shots, don't look at the ground. Roll like a boxer, don't roll like a novice – that's from the street. I need to establish my authority behind the jab, don't be countering him from two foot out, get in close, but when I counter, move my feet, counter, and then get out – little things like that. When I was fighting Dillian I was eager to just hurt him with one punch, but it's the flurry of punches that put you down at heavyweight.

'I've watched a lot of the Cuban guys because they're unbelievable with their balance and footwork, very relaxed on top, but very sharp with their feet. In my last fight I was very sharp with my upper body but too lazy with my feet, so I'm just switching that around and it's been working really well. Moving in, moving out, moving across and you always put someone in the position where your hands go and that's what I've been working on.'

He told Sky Sports News he was determined to take the title off Martin, saying, 'Even if I get that belt, I've got to separate my lifestyle of a champion to boxing because they don't really mix. Boxing is a gritty sport and you have got to be hungry. You've always got to separate the two. All the glitz and glamour and stuff – that's how I look at Charles Martin and I've got to separate him from the gold because I've got to fight Charles Martin. I'm not fighting the belt – that's just a reward and that's how I have to look at Charles Martin. He's just another opponent – like the last 15.'

Anthony was also asked what his reaction was to comments

from Tyson Fury that he was a bodybuilder, not a fighter, and that Fury would beat him. Fury had said the previous week, 'All he's got is a big punch, which everyone who pumps iron for five years and is 6ft 6ins can punch like. This game is not all about bodybuilding. It's about knowing how to box. He's getting knocked out.'

Clearly, if AJ did overcome all the boxers who were being placed before him, and Fury managed to sort himself out and return to the ring fit and well, a potential 'Battle of Britain' against Mancunian Fury could be on the cards – and could be big business given the fireworks that could spark ringside between the two men. Anthony was confident he would dispense of Fury if the fight did happen and believed Fury and his team were simply envious of his physique! AJ told reporters, 'They're hating on my beach body, they're just hating, that's what it is. If they want, I'll give them some sessions, they can come train with me if they want. I asked them to spar, they don't want to spar, they don't want to work, so they can stay there, but this is just how I am. I ain't got no comments on his physique. There's a lot of jealousy, a lot of negativity, so that's why I shut it down and just focus on myself. I don't search for their attention, I'm not worried if he backs me or not, because I'll still handle my business. He's not supposed to back me realistically, so I don't expect no different.'

I would contend that Fury did back Anthony in his battle with Charles Martin: he knew a fight against his fellow Brit would easily outsell any match-up with Martin. The big money would be with AJ, not Martin who was a relative nobody despite his good fortune in winning the IBF crown. That Fury then predicted that Martin would knock Anthony out was kidology – a quote to make the papers and to help push any fight with AJ closer still. Sources inside the boxing world said Fury, in the real world, was actually convinced that Joshua would knock Martin out, rather than the other way round. But this was the way the 'industry' worked – say what you believe will build the hype for a fight that would bring the readies home for you. It had been part of the fight game for decades, since Ali first fought Frazier and Don King worked at boosting ringside attendances and TV viewing figures, so why change a winning formula in 2016 and 2017?

David Haye also jumped on the Joshua bandwagon, saying he too believed Martin might have too much for AJ to deal with. Haye said, 'Joshua is a novice, going into a world challenge after only 15 fights. It's a huge risk, against a big-hitting southpaw. The upside is that Martin hasn't had many more fights himself and we don't know yet how good he is. The problem is that we don't really know how good Joshua is, either.' Of course, Haye did not want to be left behind as the Joshua bandwagon rolled on. If Tyson Fury was going for gold with his push for a 'Best of British' fight with Anthony, then so the bloody hell would he! It just emphasised how big AJ had become in such a short time as a pro – even seasoned pros like Fury and Haye, who many had considered *the* big cash cows of British boxing, were now eager to grab a seat on the Joshua bandwagon.

When asked if he had a message for Haye and Fury as they badgered him for a future date, he himself played the game, saying, 'Tell them to enjoy whatever time they've got left. Soon they will be coming up against someone young. Someone fresh, strong and hungry who will be giving them very big problems. Someone called AJ.'

But for now, his focus had to be on Charles Martin. The issue with the American remained that no one really knew how good he was or what sort of questions he could ask of Anthony. Some pundits pointed to his unbeaten record and the fact that he had won the title, while others said he hadn't beaten anyone world-class like AJ and that he had won the IBF crown as much by default given Fury's implosion. At least it meant Anthony had to continue to prepare for him as if he were a true champion, who could be a handful and dangerous.

As always, Anthony's preparations were meticulous. He was pushed to the limit every day in training and by the time of the bout was at his peak – ready for anything Martin could throw at him. It would be the first time that the American public had the chance to take a close look at Anthony, and Eddie Hearn set the scene for the bout when he told the Showtime pre-fight press conference how big it was being viewed in the UK, and just how far AJ had come in the boxing world. Eddie summed up the incredible impact Anthony had already made, telling the Americans they were in for a real treat, 'Anthony Joshua has broken box office records, viewing figure records consistently since his debut a couple of years ago at the same arena. On Saturday night, he looks to become the first British Heavyweight Olympic gold medallist to go on and win a world title. It's a wonderful fight between two very talented, young, big punching heavyweights, and it's the fastest selling event ever at the O2 Arena, selling 17,000 tickets in just 90 seconds. The anticipation here is on another level. You can't walk down the street without someone asking if AJ's going to do it. Expect fireworks; expect anticipation, drama, absolutely everything in a wonderful O2 Arena. And, of course, our thanks always to our host, broadcaster in the UK, Sky Sports, but also to Stephen Espinoza and Showtime. I've been telling Stephen Espinoza [Showtime's executive vice president] for a long time about Anthony Joshua, and I'm so pleased that the US public will get a chance to see him in action on Saturday night, when I believe he will become the Heavyweight Champion of the World.'

And Stephen Espinoza himself explained just what the attraction was for Showtime as far as AJ was concerned; how they viewed him as a massive star in the making. Stephen said, 'Eddie and I have been talking about Anthony for several fights now, and we're thrilled that we were able to get a deal done and host this TV debut. And we'd like to be his TV home for the remainder of his career, and that's for two reasons. One because he's obviously a very skilled and entertaining fighter, but, two, there is a wealth of good fights that can be made. That's really the recipe for a TV programmer's dream – not just to have charismatic skilled fighters, but actually have a wealth of opponents. There are a number of them, here in the US, starting with Deontay Wilder or other UK fighters – Tyson or David Haye, as well as internationally. There's really fertile ground in the heavyweight division right now.'

So if AJ could destroy Charles Martin in front of the Americans, he would be well on his way to a glittering – and prosperous – career. One beyond the wildest dreams he no doubt had as a youth with no money and no future before he found his salvation in the boxing ring. From that situation of no-hope, he was now on the brink of making millions and proving he was an athlete of the highest calibre. It was some turnaround, and one constructed from hard work, determination and natural sporting talent. From that no-hope, AJ had found redemption and was fast becoming a role model and shining example to other kids in similar predicaments.

In the final part of the Showtime press conference, Anthony told reporters he was really looking forward to the fight, and how training had been hard but enjoyable. He said, 'In my last 12 weeks in training, it's been a great camp. We've been sparring like 13 rounds, 14 rounds. It's been mental toughness, day after day. Pushing myself has been great. And then moving into the fight I've been a watching a lot of champions. One thing I've learned from them is just composure. That's what I'm going to take into this fight. So when I am in the ring I'll just deal with what I've got to face and just stay composed, I should show people that basically anything's possible. I'm an underdog. I'm a challenger that can come in and annihilate a champion. Kind of like when Tyson fought Douglas. Just don't give Charles Martin a chance and just outclass him, and that's what I want to do on Saturday.'

He also made it abundantly clear he did not expect to have problems because he was not experienced enough. He did not fear the fight lasting longer than other fights he'd had. If it did, he would cope, but he also did not anticipate it going the distance given the power of his fists, as he explained to the press, 'I think that when the red carpet's been laid out for you, you can only walk down it with the amount of experience that you have. I haven't got 200 rounds under my belt and 50 fights. I'm just the man I am. And with the cards I've got, I'm going to make the most of it. And that's how I have to attack this fight. It would have been great to have 50 fights and x amount of rounds, but I feel great with having 32 rounds and 15 fights. So, that's why I think it's all about mind-set. It's how one person looks at it and how another does.

'And I'm confident that there won't be another 12 rounds added onto this fight. It's going to stay in limited numbers, and that's not being cocky. It's just more of a confidence thing. It's the way we train in the gym – and they say the fight begins a long time before the fight. I'm so confident moving forward, because I'm hungry. I'm determined. And I just want to go in there and put on a great show. And I know he'll crumble. I just know I'm confident in making people crumble after a few rounds.'

Martin, naturally enough, disagreed with those sentiments. His final words before battle commenced suggested he believed experience *would* win the day, and that he would end Anthony's unbeaten start to his pro career. Martin told the press, 'I've got more fights than him – in the amateurs and the pros. Overall I've got more experience. It doesn't matter who you got in the ring with as a professional and fought because the experience and getting comfortable is what it's all about. I don't feel that he's comfortable enough in the ring and especially not with me being in there. When I get in there and start doing the things that I do in there, he's gone. It's going to be a different story. It's going to be a whole different look.'

It was time for the talk to stop and the action to begin. Much was at stake: a world crown, two unbeaten records and AJ's dash to the top would certainly be delayed if he fell victim to the American. But when the duo entered the ring, it was immediately clear that AJ was the favourite. He looked fit and sculpted while Martin's stomach could hardly be described in the same way. He looked a little flabby and out of condition. Either he had not taken the fight seriously enough, or he simply was not as conditioned as a serious athlete should be. One boxing writer even claimed on the night that Martin shouldn't have been in the ring as 'he was fat'.

AJ did not look at all worried when the two men met to touch gloves before the first bell. It took him just two rounds to send his opponent back to the States a beaten man, and to become a world champion in just his 16th professional fight. Martin survived just 1:32 minutes into the second round. An initial belting right hand sent him to the canvas, but he managed to get up. But when another massive right caught him seconds later, it was all over. This time Charles Martin struggled to get up but the referee parted his arms to say the bout was over. Martin was on his way home; AJ was on his way to a brilliant future with his first world belt, the IBF version, around his waist.

The home fans in the O2 were delighted that Anthony had won, but there was also a feeling that Martin had been well out of his depth. That he should never have been champion in the first place and that he was in no way a serious opponent for Anthony. Unusually for AJ, he showed a certain irritation in his post-fight reaction in the ring, scolding reporters and commentators who he guessed correctly would now suggest Martin had not been up to it in the first place. AJ said, 'I ain't gonna get too carried away. Every heavyweight has power but it's about speed. I showed him levels, I said I would. There'll probably be some negativity, people saying Martin was easy, but a few days ago he was this big dangerous southpaw. I don't take nonsense from no one, but I'm humble. All the hype is good for everyone in boxing. Get behind every boxer, not just myself. They've been calling me out since last year. I'm going to keep grinding, keep working. When I step into the ring, I'll be ready.'

In social-media posts, Martin inexplicably claimed the loss was due to 'distractions' – and then did not elaborate upon what exactly they were, and why they should have made a difference to his sluggish showing. He had posted, 'Everyone, the fight was not rigged, he was the better man that night. I was dealing with many distractions prior to it and my head was not there. Plain and simple I will be back. I am the real deal, just that night didn't prove it. My body was in the ring but mentally I was not there – sorry. And for the record anyone could have beat Charles Martin that night – sorry everyone.

'No excuses. I don't want to take away from Joshua but it just wasn't me and everyone can see that. Maybe I just took the fight too soon. My head was somewhere else. But I ain't crying over spilled milk. Congrats to Joshua but I'll be back. I will prove that was a fluke and gain another belt and see Joshua again soon. Nothing I can say will change people's minds that was not me in there – I beat myself – but I'm not one to make excuses so I'll be back.'

I would contend that the distractions were mostly in the ring – in the form of Joshua's gloves, especially the right-hand one, that brought about Martin's fall from grace. At least he took his big paycheck back to the US, but probably hoped his comments might secure a rematch – and another paycheck. But his chance had surely been and gone. Martin's 'reign' as heavyweight champion had lasted just 85 days, but at least he didn't suffer the ignominy of holding the crown for the shortest tenure. That went to Tony Tucker who, in 1987, lasted just 64 days as champ with 'Iron' Mike Tyson taking his crown.

Dillian Whyte felt that Joshua had been given a ride that was too easy by Martin, and that he had put on a much better show when he and AJ fought – which was quite true. Whyte told Sky Sports, 'Martin was terrible. I couldn't believe how terrible he was. He knew he was coming here to give his belt away so he just went to the highest bidder. Fair play to him, though – he got paid for losing his belt. It's rubbish that Joshua is punching harder – Martin is just cr*p. Martin never had the desire and the will to win. I had the desire and the will to win [against Joshua] even though I was injured in the second round. Martin never had it.'

Martin's lamentable showing even earned scorn back home in the US. Deontay Wilder, the impressive Alabama WBC heavyweight champ and the man who could pose the biggest threat to Anthony, led the chorus of disapproval, telling reporters, 'You always want to go with your countrymen. But to be honest, Martin, he disappointed us all. Not only me, but a lot of people. You could tell that he didn't want to fight no more. He could have gotten up. I think he felt he got hit harder than he's ever been hit in his career and didn't know how to mentally deal with that. He didn't want to get back up and fight. He thought about how he got the biggest payday of his career. I heard after the fight, he went home and bought a Bentley. Stuff like that, you don't get far. Now he's rated as the No. 2 second-shortest champion. I was very disappointed in him. I don't even want to talk about him any more.'

While Anthony would now go on to greater things, Charles Martin would hit another low. In the August after his defeat by AJ, he was shot in Los Angeles after getting into an argument with two men. 'I looked down and saw a pool of blood. I said to myself, I gotta get outta here,' Martin told tmz.com. 'I'm gonna die. I'm gonna bleed to death. I have to pay respect to the cops: they saved my life.'

Martin's right arm was injured in the shooting and it would be 12 months after his defeat by Anthony before he stepped inside a ring for another competitive bout. Martin would beat journeyman Byron Polley in two rounds the day before AJ fought Klitschko at the O2. Martin fought in front of a scattering of spectators at a casino while Anthony's bout with Wladimir brought in 90,000 fans at Wembley. Martin's fight was not televised – little wonder given the absolute lack of appeal – while AJ's was beamed live in the UK and featured heavily in America.

Such are the fate and fortunes awaiting the men who bravely put their bodies on the line in a trade-off for boxing glory and financial reward. The boxing game can be a cruel one if you lose focus. If ever Anthony Joshua needed a reminder of what life was like before he left behind a misspent youth to become a national sporting hero, Charles Martin's rapid fall from the big time would provide a perfect starting point. It also highlights what could lie ahead for Anthony if he ever fell back into his old ways. Not that, for one moment, I expect him to. However, Charles Martin's downfall remains a cautionary tale – and a relevant one in the Anthony Joshua story.

CHAPTER 10

THE TEAM BEHIND THE MAN

Anthony's lust for knowledge and self-development played a big part in how he set up his back-up team when he started to make it big. No way was he going to have an office-based manager he never saw hidden away somewhere in London, who made contact on the phone now and again to tell him who and where he would be fighting next. He decided he would have a strong support team, each with a defined role, who could best help him develop and make the most of his opportunities. He wanted to be a David Beckham, with merchandise and image deals and widespread appeal outside his sport, rather than a slugger who staggered from fight to fight with no targets or ambition. Anthony Joshua wanted to become British boxing's first crossover success – a fighter who transcended the pugilistic arena, whom the British public in general would come to recognise and want to know more about.

To that end, he launched his own executive team, AJ Boxing Management, in November 2015. A press statement outlined the new company's remit, 'AJ Boxing Management will exclusively represent all of his sporting and commercial commitments in and out of the ring. Anthony's new core management team will consist of company director Seyi Alabi and commercial manager Freddie Cunningham, both of whom have represented and worked with Anthony in different capacities for a number of years. To complement his team Anthony has also hired sporting publicity agency SoapBox London to look after all his personal press and all media commitments.

While Anthony explained, 'I am really excited to be moving to the next stage in my professional career. It feels like the right time to take control of all my professional and commercial commitments with a core group of people who have been with me for a long time and I trust fully. I would like to thank my previous agencies for all the work they have put in over the years. I have learned a lot and hope to put it all in to practice with AJ Boxing Management.'

The team also included a head of merchandise and operations, a chief support network officer, a boxing coach, two physios, a nutritionist, a head of security and a strength and conditioning coach. It was a professional way to run an individual boxing star and certainly a long way from Muhammad Ali's permanent line-up of trainer Angelo Dundee and promoter Don King.

Freddie Cunningham would be AJ's right-hand man, the man who did the deals and made the calls, and whom AJ describes in this way on his official website, anthonyjoshua.com: 'Freddie is responsible for the day-to-day running of Anthony's career. He heads up Anthony's management company overseeing all the aspects to Anthony's development outside of the ring. His core role involves the arrangement of all AJ's commercial activities from commercial activities from sponsors to appearances and acts as the driving force that keeps the whole machine moving forward.' With such a wide portfolio of duties and targets, Freddie was clearly the power behind the throne in the empire. Freddie said his remit was to 'work with Anthony's existing commercial partners and training team to make sure everything is being run to the highest of standards. We will also be responsible for seeking out new opportunities and business development for Anthony.'

The *Daily Mail* reported that Freddie gained a degree in business studies with marketing at Bournemouth University in 2011, and then joined PR company Pitch before entering sports management with The Sports Partnership. He moved to Sport Digital in 2015 but after six months became the commercial manager with AJ. Freddie told the *Daily Telegraph* that he and Anthony worked closely together every day, 'We'll probably speak four or five times a day and he'll come to meetings that I'm at. He likes to understand it. Everything we do with brand partnerships . . . there's a massive consideration in terms of what the output is going to look like.'

It was a young team and it helped that Anthony was good friends with the figures he would rely heavily on to ensure his assets were well looked after outside the ring, as well as in it. Seyi Alabi would, like Freddie, also continue to play a key role. An architectural designer by trade who worked for Brixton-based Stephen Crawford Architects, Seyi had a long-standing association with AJ and would continue to work with

Freddie to enhance the promotion of the boxer's image in and out of the ring. AJ's website described him thus, 'As a member of Anthony's family Seyi has been there from the start. His primary role is to advise and guide AJ on any decision he needs help with. He also consults with Freddie and Anthony on the direction AJ Boxing is moving.'

And at the formation of the new management team, Seyi said, 'This is a very important moment for Anthony, both in a sporting and professional sense. It certainly feels like the correct time for him to be launching AJ Boxing Management. We will work hard behind the scenes to make sure that commercially we can keep pace with his rapid progress in the ring.'

Another top post was that of David Ghansa, also known as KD. Anthony's website explained the trust AJ put in KD, 'One of Anthony's closest friends, KD is AJ's chief support network on a day-to-day basis, travelling with him to and from camp every week, consulting with Freddie on logistical and operational issues and also managing ticket sales for AJ's fights.'

And then there was the head of security, Ben Ilyemi, aka Benga, who receives the ultimate accolade from his cousin, AJ, 'Without Benga we may never have seen AJ in a ring. A former professional himself he was the person who took Anthony to his first-ever boxing gym. He is cousin to AJ and also his Head of Security. Meaning he is responsible for the safety of the group in and around fight week.'

Anthony even had the nous to employ the sporting publicity agency SoapBox, based in London, to look after all his personal press and media commitments. It was a clever move, and stressed how important the presentation of image was to AJ. Company co-founder Andy Bell said, 'We are thrilled to be working with Anthony, he is in a small group of professional athletes who can truly transcend their sport and become part of popular culture and we look forward to helping him with his journey.'

Iwan Llewellyn is Anthony's social media manager. Iwan, who lists France international footballer Antoine Griezmann among his clients, 'analyses the commercial value of sportsmen and sportswomen's digital platforms'.

Will Harvey would become head of merchandise and operations, or as AJ would have it, 'Responsible for the growth and development of Anthony's range of merchandise. He also assists Freddie with the day-to-day management of AJ Boxing.'

The nutritionist is Mark Ellison, described as being 'responsible for managing AJ's diet, ensuring he has enough fuel to charge his body, and the right nutrients to remain in healthy shape and condition through out a long camp'.

Jamie Reynolds has the important job of strength and conditioning coach, a role designed to steer Anthony away from sapping, worrying injuries. In his role, Jamie 'devises specific strength and dynamic drills to support Rob [McCracken] in AJ's training camp. Designed to specifically target boxing-relevant training and injury prevention.' The two physios are Rob Madden and Sina Ghami, both tasked with keeping their man in tip-top condition when the aches and pains start up, 'Sina works with AJ on a weekly basis giving him sports and deep-tissue massages to ensure that there is no muscle soreness or tightness in AJ's body at the end of a training week. His primary job is to ensure that AJ is feeling physically fresh for the start of a new week. Rob sees Anthony about 2–3 times a month to help with any niggles or injuries AJ often gets during a long, tough camp. He is responsible for keeping AJ's finely tuned body going, and hitting peak physical condition on fight night.'

And, last but certainly not least in the team, is the redoubtable Rob McCracken, AJ's boxing coach and long-time ally from the days when he represented GB as an amateur. The Joshua website describes him as 'former coach of Carl Froch and Head of GB Boxing. Rob is an extremely experienced coach and has worked with Anthony in some form throughout his whole career. Now his full-time coach, Rob works extremely closely with AJ and prepares him for every fight and leads the corner during AJ's fights.'

He is a hard taskmaster and that is probably down to his once being a boxer himself, a former middleweight who fought for the world crown. Sometimes he pushed AJ so hard that the boy admitted to feeling like laying one on him! Anthony told the boxing writer Pat Sheehan, 'I get angry quite easy when I am tired from training. I get angry with Rob because he pushes me all the time. When he is telling me I am doing things wrong, I want to give him a left hook to see if it is really that bad. He says it is bad and I am thinking, "I want to miss the pad here and crack and see." But you have to just control yourself and that is the discipline of boxing. You have to stay level-headed even when you want to lose your head."

Anthony said Rob CAN take a punch, though. He revealed: 'Kal Yafai, the [British] light-bantamweight world champion, was doing a session with Rob the other day. He told me he lost all confidence because he missed the pad and hit Rob with a right hand and he was just standing there.'

He might have felt like hitting him now and again, but Anthony was under no illusion whatsoever about the importance of Rob in his organisation. McCracken had pushed him to the limit and made it clear that the sky was the limit if he listened, learned and always worked as hard as he possibly could in training. AJ knew that Rob delivered – he had, after all, helped him to that Olympic gold. And he was confident that with Rob in his corner he could go all the way in the professional world heavyweight division. That he could indeed become world champion, and win every belt to unify the division.

Rob officially joined Team AJ on 1 December 2016. Anthony explained to the press pack in more detail exactly why the coach had moved for him. He said, 'I have remained close to Rob and the GB Boxing squad since 2012. I have consistently turned to him for advice and guidance so I am really excited to have him in my corner, starting on December 10. I would like to put on record my thanks to Tony Sims who will remain in my corner working with Rob as he did to such success with Carl Froch.'

McCracken, then aged 48, admitted he was excited at the prospect of working with Anthony and made it clear he felt that their link-up would make big waves in the world of boxing. He would remain with the GB squad and was confident that the dual role would have benefits for both AJ and his Olympic hopefuls, who would see AJ training at Sheffield. Rob said, 'Anthony is a special talent. I am looking forward to working with him on the next stage of his career as he looks to defend his titles and, ultimately, to unify the heavyweight division. I know from working with Carl Froch that combining my work coaching a top professional boxer with the role of performance director has mutual benefits and that having a world champion in the gym has a very positive impact on the whole of the GB Boxing squad. It gives the boxers an insight into what it takes to be the best in the world and provides top-class training opportunities that will help to develop and improve the heavyweight and super-heavyweight boxers in the squad.'

The recruitment of McCracken would prove to be a masterstroke. It would give Anthony an extra edge as Rob pushed him to the absolute edge every day in training. Rob imparted his knowledge of the fight game to his student and Anthony listened and learned. He had no doubt that this man knew what he was talking about; he had been in the fight game at the top end himself. He had walked the walk and so was entitled to talk the talk as what he said was sure to help AJ's development. McCracken ironed out the raw edges that Anthony had not sorted from his amateur days and instilled in him the need to be absolutely professional in all areas of his life that touched on his boxing career. That meant good training, good sleep and a good diet. Especially when they were preparing for a bout, although Rob was a proponent of living the right way always if you wanted to make the top of the boxing world – and stay there. There was no room for complacency, doubts, or complaints that this or that was too hard or too rigid.

And, to be fair, Anthony was an A-class student who worked his butt off and kept on the straight and narrow because he was determined to reach the peak of his profession. Team AJ was complete with the 'capture' of Rob McCracken. The trainer complemented the rest of the management team AJ had put together and the world was, literally, now in his hands.

Of course, there was another essential element to his success

– and that was getting the best man to put on his biggest bouts. Luckily, he had already sorted that before putting together his new management team. Anthony had already set himself up with a top-class promoter to steer the ship towards the biggest and best fights and TV deals. In July 2013, AJ went for Eddie Hearn to promote his fights and it proved to be absolutely the right decision. On the day he announced his new management line-up, Anthony also revealed that he had signed a new three-year deal with Eddie's Matchroom Boxing company.

Eddie is the son of Barry Hearn, the man who took charge of the world's best snooker players in the 1980s. In 1982 Barry set up Matchroom Sport Ltd and developed a stable of top snooker stars, as well as producing TV events. Matchroom snooker players included Terry Griffiths, Dennis Taylor, Willie Thorne, Neal Foulds, Jimmy White, Cliff Thorburn and Ronnie O'Sullivan.

Barry moved into boxing at the end of the decade and was the man who put on hundreds of bouts, and not just domestic ones. In his time, he organised British, European and World title clashes. His first big promotion was the Frank Bruno versus Joe Bugner fight at White Hart Lane in October 1987. It would propel Barry into the big league of boxing promoters after he stepped in to put on the bout when Bruno's fight against American Trevor Berbick was cancelled 11 days before it was due to go ahead at Wembley.

Bruno was ready for a bout and Barry came up with the idea of pitting him against the long-time pantomime villain of British boxing, Joe Bugner, who was by then based in Australia. The *Daily Mirror* highlighted how big the project could be by saying, 'It could be ON. The heavyweight punch-up every fight fan in

Britain wants to see – the showdown between Frank Bruno and Joe Bugner.' It was a quite brilliant move by Barry, a match-up the public wanted and were eager to see. Tickets sold quickly and a 40,000 sell-out was expected as the match would not be shown live on TV.

But Barry would then make headline news for something not to his advantage. He had vowed the fight would not be live on TV but later arranged for it to be shown an hour after the first bell. Now the *Daily Mirror* turned on him, accusing him of 'double-crossing' all the punters who had forked out to watch it live at the Lane, 'Britain's fight fans have been pulled on to a monster "sucker punch" by boxing's newest promoter, Barry Hearn. He pledged that the eagerly-awaited £3 million heavyweight punch-up between Frank Bruno and Joe Bugner at White Hart Lane on Saturday would NOT be screened live by TV. But now, I understand, ITV will show the clash of the boxing juggernauts at 10.30 p.m. Strictly speaking, Hearn has lived up to his pledge. Just. By precisely seven minutes if the twelve round scrap, scheduled to start at 9.35, goes the distance.' For his part, Barry replied, 'I don't think the public has been conned. I believe real fight fans will want to be there as it actually happens. If the TV screening has been delayed by an hour it's not live, and I think sports fans understand and expect it. They know that is sport in 1987.'

Had Barry done wrong? The fight was, after all, only to be shown when the bout itself had finished. And if you go by the old adage that 'all publicity is good publicity' he certainly had made a name for himself. In his first pro fight for Matchroom he was the talk of Britain's clubs and pubs. And he had shown he could stage the biggest of events, even at the first time of asking. As a sidenote, Bruno won the bout by a knockout, much to the delight of the thousands of fans who dreamed of 'Aussie Joe' taking a battering.

So Barry's son Eddie had much to live up to after the decisive path laid down by his illustrious father. Barry had been a pioneer in the way he had brought that first fight to a sell-out crowd at White Hart Lane and also sold it to television. He had proved that he could put on a show that would pull in the punters and leave them wanting more. Now would his son be able to match his success, or would it be a step too far? Yet that gauntlet seemed to serve only to inspire Eddie to graft harder and to pull out every stop to prove he could do just that. He did not take the easy route to the top; indeed he had a hunger to show that he was his own man, and that he wouldn't be a success just because of who his father was. It was this drive that brought him to Anthony's attention – drive, and a willingness to listen and help his young charge.

Even when he was studying in his teens, Eddie proved he was not afraid to get his hands dirty. After a day of learning, he would do a shift for a double-glazing firm to try to earn a few quid, as he told the *Guardian* in April 2017: 'I worked for Weatherseal in Romford. I'd go there after college at night and do telesales. It's the worst job in the world but the best training for sales. For every rejection we had an answer on a list . . . we always had a reason to make an appointment. I was on £3 an hour but for every appointment you got a £5 bonus and your money went up by £1 an hour. So every booking was worth £7. But then I did work experience for dad at 17. I was selling sponsorship in fight magazines, which was a doddle compared to phoning some geezer about double-glazing who says, "F***off, I don't want to talk to you."'

For several years, he would work in the sponsorship and event management industry, before eventually joining Matchroom Sport in 2000 with responsibility for the newly formed Matchroom Golf management business. In 2005, he assumed the role of Chief Executive of the PGA Europro Tour and subsequently headed up Matchroom Sport's poker and online gaming operations. Now Group Managing Director, he had earned the right to be the top man on his own terms, not because he was Barry's son. It would have been the easy option to join his dad's operation early in an executive role but he served his apprenticeship, gaining vital experience away from the family firm. It was this work ethic and easy-going yet determined outlook to be the best that appealed to Anthony when he was looking for a promoter.

It also helped that Eddie had made positive inroads into the world of TV for his boxing stable. Anthony could see that this was a man who would not only get him the right fights at the right time, but would also get him the right kind of coverage. In 2015, it was revealed that Matchroom had signed an exclusive six-year deal with Sky Sports for UK and Irish rights; a deal that would bring 120 nights of live boxing. And, as Sky were keen to point out, 'Viewers will also be able to watch gold medallist Anthony Joshua MBE, one of Britain's most exciting sporting prospects.'

Eddie summed up the partnership's benefit for AJ and his other fighters, saying, 'I am delighted to announce a new five-year deal as Sky's exclusive boxing promoter in the UK and Ireland. Over the past three years, with Sky Sports' backing, we have developed a team of fighters unrivalled by any promotional company in the history of British boxing. We have worked together to take British boxing from small-hall shows to filling major arenas all over the country, creating star attractions and taking the profile of the sport to another level. Without Sky Sports consistent backing of British boxing over the years, none of this would have been possible and as we approach a golden era for our sport, it makes me proud to provide such an elite team of fighters with the opportunity to achieve their dreams on the UK's number 1 sporting platform.'

Not that Eddie ever became complacent. His reputation and hard-earned cash were always on the line when he set up a fight. The costs involved were massive and he was aware that he could have problems if the shows did not sell, as he told the *Daily Mail* in an excellent interview in May 2016: 'If a fighter sells 200 tickets at £50 that is about 10 grand to the show. If I'm paying two guys £1,500 each to be bottom of the card, that is £3,000 so 10 grand in ticket sales means £7,000 profit from one guy alone But if you are one of the bigger guys and the fight is costing me 10 grand but you are selling only £1,000 of tickets, that doesn't sound great. It might still be worth it because you are investing in a good fighter's future, building his profile. That is a massive part of what we do – building financially viable cards but also selling the right fighters. If a guy doesn't sell or fight well, you're pretty f*****. If he sells and fights well, that's gold dust.'

Eddie's achievement was to take boxing from traditionally

small halls to major arenas on a regular basis – and that was the kind of initiative Anthony wanted in a promoter for his burgeoning boxing career. To step out in the likes of the O2 and Wembley to show what he could do, and constantly expand his audience base. With Eddie Hearn at the helm, he was certain he would do just that, plus he liked the guy as a person, which is always useful! The pair would talk for hours and AJ told pals he felt totally at ease chatting with him, knowing anything that was shared would stay between the two of them. Like his dad, Eddie would also become a high-profile character within boxing, appearing on boxing media channels with interviews about upcoming bouts, and was a regular tweeter on social media, where he had 513,000 followers. AJ had made a good choice in one of the key roles in his management team: Eddie Hearn could be relied on to help take him to the next level.

As Anthony said of Eddie at the start of their link-up, 'Eddie's bringing a new era to boxing. I know boxers that have gone with Eddie Hearn that haven't got a bad word to say about him.'

And that was why he was so happy to sign another deal with him at the end of November, 2015. Sky, naturally, were as delighted as Eddie that AJ would be staying with him – as it also meant he would be staying with them under the six-year deal Eddie had signed with them earlier that year. Sky showed their delight with a breezy statement, 'The Olympic gold medallist has raced to 14–0 in the professional ranks with 14 devastating KOs under the guidance of promoter Eddie Hearn, and has penned the new deal prior to headlining his first Sky Sports Box Office event event on 12 December at the O2 in London, where he faces bitter rival Dillian Whyte for the British and Commonwealth titles.'

Anthony was also pleased at the new contract, saying, 'I have been part of the Matchroom family for a number of years now and I am really excited that the relationship will be continuing. They have an exceptional and passionate team from Eddie downwards. Matchroom have provided me with the perfect platform to get my professional career started and there was never a question that they were the guys, with Sky Sports, to help move me to the next level and ultimately to a shot at the heavyweight world championship.'

And Eddie was similarly enthusiastic, adding, 'The first two years [since he and AJ signed their initial contract] have been a great experience and I feel the journey has been faultless both in and out of the ring. Anthony's profile has continued to grow and he has boxed in virtually every major city in the UK but, more importantly, those experiences coupled with tremendous dedication in the gym have seen him develop immensely as a fighter. Anthony has already become one of the hottest commodities in world sport and we are blessed with the responsibility of helping to guide Anthony Joshua to the world heavyweight title and ultimately unifying the division.'

You could perhaps argue that Eddie's description of AJ as 'a commodity' was a bit below the belt, but Eddie is a businessman as well as a listener and friend to Anthony. He had to assess that the figures always add up and Anthony is more than happy with that side of their relationship. He does not want him or his team to get a raw deal when he is literally putting his body and well-being on the line every time he gets in that ring. So the link-up with a man he liked and trusted was intrinsically ideal. The duo would now go from strength to strength as they worked together; both on the same winning wavelength.

THE DREAM CATCHER

Following his emphatic defeat of Charles Martin, Anthony took a couple of weeks' breather to come back down to earth, recharge his batteries and unwind. Training for world-title fights is demanding and requires all a fighter's time, concentration, and physical and mental energy. After such a fight, boxers tell of the low that invariably follows the high if you win, and the even greater low that comes with defeat. For Anthony, it would be like popping a balloon as he experienced the ecstasy of lifting that first world crown, succeeded by the sudden deflation and inevitable physical slump that follows that moment when you have given everything to attain your dream, leaving you drained. He wasn't depressed, just temporarily tired and urgently in need of rest. So for a couple of weeks, he made time to be with his family, took things easy and returned to normality, playing his Playstation and laughing and joking with friends.

But then it was time to refocus. Such is the life of a top athlete nowadays. AJ is no boozer anyway and always watches what he eats, so it was not as though he was out of condition or would need a drastic boot camp to lose weight. He had never had to battle the flab, like some boxers, and always maintained his sculpted physique with weights and gym work, even when unwinding. But the fact was that less than three months after he had beaten Charles Martin to lift the IBO world heavyweight title, he had been lined up for his first defence of that title. So after the short unwinding session, he would need to up his fitness and begin again the gruelling workouts needed to ensure he was in tip-top condition for a fight.

Furthermore, the man Eddie Hearn had lined up for him to make that first defence against was no bum. No, he was another American and a boxer who, on paper at least, looked as if he might put in a heavier shift than had Charles Martin – that he might trouble Anthony, or at least take him beyond the usual two-round destructions. Dominic Breazeale was four years older than AJ, but his credentials suggested that he was a good prospect. Like Anthony, he was successful in other sports as well as boxing. It was claimed he might have made a career in American football, just as AJ had been touted to become a professional footballer. Dominic had been a quarterback for the team at the University of Northern Colorado, and had starred for the team, known as 'The Bears', in 2006 and 2007, before turning to boxing. At 6 foot 7 inches and lean and mean, he was the closest thing to a mirror image that Anthony had faced since turning pro. Breazeale, born in Alhambra, California, had switched to boxing in November 2012.

He would later learn that the switch maybe wasn't as surprising as it may have initially seemed to his family and his friends. His mother, Tina, had died, and after her sad passing he had opened boxes in her home, which led to an unexpected discovery. He found boxing paraphernalia belonging to his biological father, whom he hardly knew. There was a Golden Gloves state-championship belt, boxing shoes, a mouthguard, and news articles telling the story of his dad's boxing career. Harold Lee Breazeale had been a successful amateur fighter, and suddenly his own destiny became clearer to Dominic.

He told the *LA Times*, 'I have the pedigree, and I didn't even know it. I guess it's natural to me. It's in my blood. I never built a relationship with him like I did with my stepfather, Terry, who was there from Day One and raised me as a man, getting me ready for life.' But while Terry had looked after him and been there for him, Harold had been absent – locked up in prison for most of Dominic's life.

His father's incarceration also helped Dominic to understand why his mother had been so against him going into boxing – she told him he should stick to football and basketball, and forget about the fight game. No doubt she had feared it might lead her son on to the same path that his wayward biological dad had followed.

He would tell reporters, 'I remember telling my mom, "Hey, there's these kids going to this local gym. They put on some gear, get in the boxing gym and literally beat the heck out of each other, and when they get out of the ring, they're the best of friends, high-fiving. I want to join." There was no explanation, just a, "No, you're not doing it." She was a huge supporter of what I do, but she wanted to keep me away from boxing. It sucks that I can't ask her now, but she did it for a beneficial reason, I'm sure. If she knew I was going to become a 2012 US Olympian, go on and fight for the IBF title, become the next heavyweight champ, she would have started me like every other sport at five or six years old.'

Breazeale, who has three sons, added, 'It took until my fifth or sixth professional fight for her to come and watch me live. I had to ask other family members about it [his dad's career], and they were surprised I'd no idea. There I am seven years into boxing and nobody told me my father was a standout amateur.'

Breazeale won the 2012 US National Super Heavyweight championship at the Fort Carson Special Events Center in Colorado. He was being mentored by Michael King, the CEO of a company called All American Heavyweights, whose aim was to help Dominic win gold at the Olympics to be held in London later that year. King was delighted his boy had won the championship at Colorado and believed it augured well for the Olympics.

Just as Team GB had a boxing centre of excellence in Sheffield, so King had set up a similar hi-tech, state-of-the-art facility called The Rock, in Carson, near Los Angeles. It was fortunate for Breazeale and the other American boxing hopefuls that King encouraged them to use his facilities, as funding had been cut for the Olympics team. And Breazeale was even more fortunate because he had been personally funded by King since 2008.

He had trained at the Rock since it opened that year and was viewed as the Golden Boy of the US Olympics team. King was paying him a monthly stipend of $3,500 and another

$1,000 toward his rent, according to the reliable *USA Today*. And Dominic was certainly confident of his own ability, saying, 'There are 14 superheavyweights signed up for London. I like to think of it as me and 13 victims.'

He would also tell *USA Today*, 'If you asked me three and a half years ago if I could be the heavyweight champion of the world, I'd say, "No way. You're crazy," If you ask me now, I'd say, "Definitely. Put me in the ring. Let's go."'

King was also sure that Breazeale would repay his generosity with gold in London, saying, 'He's 6-7, 255 . . . and ripped! I think there's our gold medallist. Isn't it amazing how fast he moves for a big guy?" Anthony Joshua and Breazeale would first cross paths at the Games in London that summer of 2012.

But they would not meet in the ring. No, while AJ was heading towards the gold medal, Dominic crashed out in the first round, losing to the impressive Russian, Magomed Omarov, 19–8. As the scoreline would suggest, the American was trounced by an opponent who made his experience and know-how count. The boxing website, badlefthook.com, best summed up his defeat, commenting, 'Absolute destruction as the wheels fall off of Team USA with their fifth straight loss. Totally outclassed was Breazeale, which was frankly expected. The former Northern Colorado quarterback is a baby in the sport and it showed. Omarov hurt him and put it on him throughout the fight, but Breazeale showed a lot of guts hanging in with a far better fighter.'

It was a fine analysis, and one that suggested that Dominic *could* yet develop into a fine boxer if he did turn professional. He was brave and would only improve with time and more bouts and rounds under his belt. That belief would be backed up by his impressive record as he jetted over to England to take on AJ at the O2 Arena on 25 June 2016. From 9 November 2012, he had notched 17 consecutive wins, 14 of them KO's. That compared favourably with Anthony's record of 16 KO's in his 16 fights. Dominic had beaten fellow American Curtis Lee Tate in that first bout, the fight not lasting one round. Almost six months before he met AJ, he had notched his 17th win at the Staples Centre in LA. Another American, Amir Mansour, was his victim, retiring in the fifth round.

The victory over Mansour provided him with his first title – the vacant WBC Continental Americas heavyweight crown. But it was by no means a straightforward demolition: Breazeale suffered the first knockdown of his career and allowed his opponent the opportunity to breach his defences on several occasions. The fight was stopped in Round 5 over fears Mansour had suffered a broken jaw, but Anthony, watching on TV in England, would not have become suddenly fearful of the man who would be his next opponent. He would have noted how Mansour hit Dominic with a bomb of a right hand at the start of the third round, and how it felled him. That would no doubt be one of his plans of action.

But he would also have noted, as had often been said of Breazeale, that he was a brave fighter who never gave in. Plenty of men would have stayed on the canvas after that right hand assault by Mansour, but Dominic had the guts to get up and continue. He survived by clinging on to the ropes and holding on to his opponent. Clearly he had a big heart, but he also then showed the power and ability to turn the contest around as he bombarded Mansour with shots to the face, forcing him to retire, his mouth bleeding, in the fifth.

In America, the general feeling among boxing fans was that Joshua and Breazeale would be a good fight, in that they were evenly matched with strong knockout figures and in that they were both relatively inexperienced yet promising. One fan in the States commented: 'What do we really know about Anthony Joshua? He beat unknown Charles Martin, Dillian Whyte and the world's most boring fighter Kevin Johnson. Kid has had 16 impressive fights but he is not a world champion. The world champion is Tyson Fury until someone beats him – so Anthony Joshua can fight whoever he wants. Let's just be grateful that he's not taking on veteran Owen Beck or someone of that calibre.

'Dominic Breazeale is a very good opponent and I am surprised that Anthony is fighting someone this dangerous. Dominic may not have looked too impressive in his last fights but the man has great power, a great chin and has never lost. Dominic isn't someone who Joshua can put away with just one shot. He also isn't someone that will be intimidated by Joshua's power. I am interested in seeing this fight. If Joshua is going to become a legendary boxer it will show against Breazeale. If it doesn't show then Joshua will end up as a win on Tyson Fury's ultra boring record – and will be remembered as someone who took part in the torturous years of the boring Fury reign.'

Fury was clearly no favourite among the Americans who regularly tuned in to the fight nights on TV. Like the Klitschkos', his name had become synonymous with a dull era in heavyweight boxing. Thankfully, the era of Anthony Joshua and, maybe, Deontay Wilder in the States, was going to change all that. AJ was ready to breathe new life into the stagnant carcass of world heavyweight boxing, and Dominic Breazeale was lined up to become his latest victim and, if all went to plan, the penultimate one before a massive bout against Wladimir Klitschko.

Breazeale was his own worst enemy when he arrived in London before the fight in June 2016. He told Sky Sports he did not believe that Anthony had deserved the gold at the Olympics, where he himself had flopped. He suggested it was only down to 'hometown judges' that AJ had triumphed. He said, 'Roberto Cammarelle, the Italian, he won that gold medal. Fighting in your back yard leaving things up to the judges, you're going to get that nod. That's why I don't plan on letting that fight on June 25 go to the judges. I do not believe Anthony Joshua is a gold medallist. Cammarelle won that fight.'

He also dismissed Anthony's destruction of Charles Martin as nothing special, adding, 'Being an American citizen watching another American go overseas and fight in the UK and fight against Anthony Joshua I was a little upset at the performance he put together in that four minutes of shame.

'I think Anthony Joshua broke more of a sweat in the back locker room then he did in the four minutes of fighting. Charles Martin wasn't good enough to be a heavyweight contender, never mind a title holder.'

If Breazeale had planned to rile Anthony, those words would surely do the job. He was basically saying Anthony was a sham who didn't deserve his Olympic gold and that his IBF title win over Martin was nothing to shout about. It was Anthony's first title defence and he viewed Breazeale's confidence as bordering on arrogance. This had been highlighted even earlier when the two fighters had come face to face for a photo opportunity, during which Anthony had felt the American was showing him a lack of respect by declining his handshake. Promoter Eddie Hearn admitted he was surprised at how angry AJ was – outside the ring he was renowned for always being cool and calm. But Hearn revealed, 'AJ was chilled and they squared up. Anthony went to shake his hand and he pushed his hand down and squared up to him out of the blue. I've not really seen Joshua lose his rag before – even before the Dillian Whyte fight – and that was the first time I've seen it.

'Breazeale is very confident. He's got the schooling that Charles Martin never had. Nobody really knew anything about Martin and that was the concern for us – an undefeated heavyweight who'd come from nowhere. Breazeale has pedigree and the way he talks shows you he's been around it. He's not fazed.'

Breazeale then shot his mouth off at a press conference organised by Matchroom Boxing, at which he told reporters that he was the underdog, but that he would emerge triumphant after the fight and would dish out heavy punishment during it. He boasted to reporters, 'I plan on putting on some extreme pressure and taking Joshua to places he's never been. We'll find out on Saturday night if he can handle it. I want him to feel uncomfortable at all given times of the fight, every second of every round. Yes, he's got rid of a lot of his guys in the earlier rounds – he hasn't been taken into deep waters.

'I'm going in as the underdog, I'm going into an arena with 17,000 opposing fans. I've been picked as the smaller guy in the ring, by the IBF as a stepping stone and I feel like my back is against the wall. I'm going to come out fighting.'

If all that wasn't enough, he continued the 'big I am' talk right up to the bout itself, even boasting during the final pre-fight press conference that he would KO Anthony. Smiling, he told reporters, 'He's seen I'm ready to go. I'm ready for it to happen. This is the biggest fight of my life and I've worked damn hard to get here. I'm embracing the big occasion and enjoying every moment of it. Without a doubt, I will inflict the first defeat of Joshua's pro career. I've got a big right hand, a big left hook and I'm unorthodox. I'm a guy that can fight on the inside, can take a punch and can give a punch. Any one of those given things shows up on the night, I'm getting a knockout for sure. As much as it's a physical game, it's a mental game as well and I've got to take advantage of both. I stared him out [when they met pre-fight], definitely. He's not physically shown it, but mentally he's rattled a little bit.'

Anthony wasn't falling for his hype – he even claimed he was more scared of spiders than the threat Dominic posed, telling reporters, 'I'm terrified of creepy crawlies. Can't stand them near me. Ugh. Hate them. Just the thought of a spider really gets under my skin. Apart from the bugs and the nasties, the only other thing I'm afraid of is losing. For me it's been business as usual. Sleep, eat, train, repeat.

'Dominic is always so tense. I asked him why and he goes, "Brother, I'm getting myself into something I'm ready for." He told me there's a new lion in town, so I explained he's coming into MY jungle. I am not saying I have got in his head but I knew what I was doing. I told him to chill out, make sure he had a good time and put on a good show. I let him know what he was in for but in a very calming way. I didn't need to rare up, I subtly let him know I'm going to knock him the f*** out.'

Anthony's humility also shone through. He was clearly not happy with some of the stuff Breazeale was spouting and had hit back by saying he would knock him out. But he also admitted he would pray for a successful outcome with trainer Tony Sims, even though he was not religious. He told the press conference, 'With stuff like entertainment and reality TV, it's easy to get caught up and lost. Prayer is a method practised from ancient days and it's very important for us to maintain a spiritual connection. It's something gladiators would do years ago anyway, so we're just maintaining that routine really. Tony leads the prayer. It's mainly for a successful night and to come out healthy. I can't remember every prayer but I'm sure he has mentioned my opponents in the past and asked for us to be watched over.

'I feel religion is a big part of life, whether you believe in it or not. I don't have a religion, I just have faith and am spiritual. Praying is a form of meditation. It's putting your thoughts out into the universe.'

Again, it showed a side of Anthony Joshua that is unusual in a heavyweight boxing champion. Not since the days of Muhammad Ali had a champ spoken with such intelligence or spiritual leaning. I will return to comparisons between the two in a later chapter, but AJ's thoughts showed he has the ability to be much more than just a boxer when he eventually decides to hang up his gloves. He had wasted his education but was making up for it in his late 20s, with the books he read and the beliefs he expounded. It was good to see him trash the idea of a boxer being a chump, rather than a champ in more ways than just a king in the ring.

Dominic Breazeale would get riled when the press continually asked him about Charles Martin, implying that he might fold like his fellow American. He replied, 'Everybody keeps comparing me to Charles Martin, but the only thing that we have in common is that we're both American. We have a completely different fight style, different goals in life. I'm a big puncher, so is Anthony Joshua. He has the belt and I intend to have it on Saturday night. I've worked damn hard to get here and I won't let this opportunity pass me by.'

Anthony had the last words before the bout – and they must have sounded ominous to Breazeale, 'He's the dangerman at the moment and so I am taking him very seriously. I've watched his fights but I won't pay too much attention to them because for this one he'll give 50 per cent more effort. I'm sure he will have prepared well. He has potential, but I have to put an end to his dream. That is why they call me "The Dream Catcher".'

So true, too. After seven rounds, Dominic Breazeale's dream of taking Anthony's IBF crown back home to America had turned into a living nightmare. He took a pounding in each round and by the end of the fight could not see out of one eye, and had semi vision in the other. To his credit, he showed immense bravery sticking in there for seven rounds. Other boxers may have hit the canvas and stayed there given the punishment being meted out to him. But not this American boy. He worked hard, got a few shots beyond AJ's defence and deserved his paycheck and the kudos of having gone so many rounds with the Dream Catcher. Dominic still had a future: he was fit, not fat like many heavyweights, and was a grafter. He deserved more big fights, but it was doubtful whether he would take on Anthony Joshua again. The Watford boy was in a different league and would have bigger fish to fry.

The end for Breazeale came in the seventh when Anthony went on the attack and battered him into a corner, the final punch being a punishing left hook that had the referee rushing over to stop AJ inflicting yet more damage. After the bout, Breazeale said, 'That was a tough fight. But I didn't suffer any concussion and I feel OK. I didn't put too many punches together and that was probably my downfall. Hopefully, I'll get another crack at him – there's some things that worked for me. But for now it's back to the drawing board. One loss isn't going to hold me down.'

Anthony walked back to his dressing room with no major bruises on his face or body. He was calm and relaxed and even had time to have a word with chef Gordon Ramsay and his son Jack. Message to Ramsay – let the boy at least get his gloves off and take a shower before you impose on him. Ramsay and son, both chewing gum furiously, didn't even have the nous to make a quick exit after being introduced. Three minutes in, Ramsay posed a defining question to AJ, 'What time did you get up this morning?' Then the duo had to have a pic taken with Anthony, chef on one side, son on the other. AJ, still sweating from the fight, hadn't even had time to cool down, gather his thoughts or unwind to the sounds of Eminem in the background. Talk about kitchen nightmares . . . this was a dressing-room nightmare. Yet, as always, Anthony was generous with his time, welcoming and friendly.

Lennox Lewis took time out to tweet his regard for the way Anthony had boxed, saying, 'Big up to Anthony Joshua on a solid win. Looked great with jab, speed, power and patience! Well done!'

That meant a lot to Anthony, especially as his meeting with Breazeale had been the first heavyweight bout since the sad death of Muhammad Ali. Tribute had been paid to 'the greatest' before the fight as ten bells tolled, and Ali's image was shown on the big screens inside the O2 Arena.

Anthony had made a successful first defence of his title and tweeted his appreciation for his opponent's bravery, 'Respect for Dom for coming out to the Lions' Den. UK we raised the roof.'

He had earlier said, 'The fight was a matter of timing and process. I didn't want to take any haymakers on the way back. I only had two weeks off after my last fight and now I want to have a nice bit of time off. I need to rest. I'm tired and I'm working hard. Now I can recharge my batteries and start afresh again.'

Eddie Hearn was also at pains to insist that AJ now took time off, away from training and fights. He said, 'He needs a long rest. He needs to go and be a young boy, go and sit on the beach with his mates and mess around. It's been absolutely relentless.'

But who would Anthony like to take on next – after he had taken that well-earned rest? He said, 'I was really looking at Tyson Fury. I hope he gets better soon, as I was hoping to get that sometime in the winter if everything went well. We're going to have to reschedule that and look at other opponents like [New Zealander] Joseph Parker if he's vacant or anybody else that the people want. I'm in a good position. Wilder, Fury, Haye, Any one of them, and they all want me.'

But it wouldn't be any of them. In the event, Anthony would

face one final test outside the 'big guns'. His final bout before what would be a massive fight against Wladimir Klitschko would see another American, Texas hardman Eric Molina, roll into the UK. He and AJ would do battle at the Manchester Arena on 10 December 2016, in the second defence of the latter's IBF title.

The really big time was close, but patience was needed from Anthony and his fans – he had to beat Molina to earn the right to fight one of the greatest heavyweights of all time. To earn the right to have his own name printed in the record books, as the man who beat the big Ukrainian and began his own era of domination in the heavyweight division. Only Molina remained in Anthony Joshua's way – but he had to be beaten or the dream of a new empire might crumble away.

CHAPTER 12

LAST MAN STANDING

One man stood in the way of Anthony Joshua and a fight with Ukrainian legend Wladimir Klitschko: Eric Molina. AJ had known he was close to the fight that would, if he won, propel him to superstardom. But he was only perilously close because if he lost to Molina all bets would be off. He would be forced to start again, climb the ladder again, back to the pinnacle – hopefully – and another chance against the kings of the heavyweight arena. But that could take a couple of years and Klitschko could be in retirement. So there was a hell of a lot resting on Anthony disposing of the Texan. The deal was signed and the bout would take place at Manchester Arena, two weeks before Christmas in 2016.

Anthony did not need telling how important the fight was. It was like a final reckoning, and one he had to win. Defeat was unthinkable and so he went about his business as if he were about

189

to fight Klitschko now, not at some time in the more distant future. His training was immaculate, he put in all the necessary hours and took all the necessary punishment in the gym and on the road. He did not complain. Eddie Hearn had stressed to him that there was no room for error and by December he was ready for action. Indeed, he was raring to go, keen to KO his opponent and make the final step to worldwide stardom which a fight with Klitschko would bring.

Molina could have presented a challenge. His record was a more than respectable 25 wins in 28 fights, with 19 knockouts. He had been fighting for a decade and was respected within the boxing world as a true pro who always gave it his best shot. His first bout, in March 2007, had ended in defeat at the hands of fellow American Ashanti Jordan in Nevada. But he pulled himself together after that loss and won his next 18 bouts. Initially a cruiserweight, he stepped up a weight and put in some impressive showings in the heavyweight arena.

In May 2014, he triumphed in what many critics in America considered his greatest career win, when he beat former world heavyweight title contender DaVarryl Williamson in five rounds. Williamson's nickname is the not particularly flattering, 'A Touch of Sleep', and Molina put him to sleep that night in Los Angeles.

Just over a year later, Molina took on the American who many pundits believe poses the biggest threat to Anthony Joshua – Deontay Wilder. The fight in Birmingham, Alabama, was Wilder's first defence of his WBC title and some believed it would be a walk in the park for him. It did not turn out that way – Molina rocked him with some powerful punches and a determination to survive. He was brave and game and Wilder knew he had been in a fight at the end of the night. It ended in the ninth round when Wilder caught him with a brutal right hand.

But Wilder admitted he had been tested – and well tested. Speaking in the ring afterwards, he said, 'To be honest, I definitely was surprised. It does my heart so good even just standing right here in front of him to say, "This guy has got heart." All of the critics doubted him. All the naysayers said he wasn't here to last, but I'm so proud of him and he has my support.

'Because this is the first title defence of any weight division in Alabama, I needed a tough guy that had heart. I needed a guy that was going to get dropped and still get up and fight and I got that out of Eric Molina. I respect him and I thank him for the opportunity to come, accept the challenge and put on a great show for the state of Alabama.'

Molina then added, 'I told you I was going to come in and give everything I'd got, and I did.'

Then came the fight that would propel Eric into Joshua's territory. In April 2016, he fought and beat Tomasz Adamek at the Krakow Arena in Poland. That win earned Molina the IBF Intercontinental heavyweight title and spelled the end for Polish legend Adamek, who had hoped for a better outcome in his homeland. The fight ended for Adamek when Molina caught him with a powerful right hand at the end of the tenth round. It was lucky for Molina that he had such a big punch in reserve because he had been behind 88-83 on the scorecards, and was heading for a defeat that would have scuppered his fight with Anthony. As it was, it was Adamek whose career was over – he now announced his retirement after 17 years in the ring and a record of 50 wins, 5 losses. No disgrace whatsoever with those sorts of figures.

For Molina, he was happy and on a high – his big pay day had arrived with the Joshua fight. As the count down to the bout in Manchester began, many pundits claimed Molina could provide a severe test for Anthony. Even AJ's promoter Eddie Hearn warned of the dangers of underestimating him, telling the BBC, 'Molina can hurt any heavyweight, and Joshua is no exception. Joshua is happy to sign for the Klitschko fight, but it would be a terrible mistake for him to start thinking about him; preparations for that fight; where it's going to be; where the training camp's going to be. Anthony won't let himself give even five per cent of his focus to Klitschko until his hand is raised in Manchester.'

That was how it should be, and how, as already outlined at the start of this chapter, journalists, fans and pros expected him to prepare. This could be far from a walk in the park – Molina was the underdog, for sure, but he had a puncher's chance of causing a major upset – and wrecking Anthony's best-laid plans for the big Klitschko showdown.

Deontay Wilder was also convinced Molina would be no pushover, having fought and beaten him. 'Molina will be a challenge for Joshua,' he said. 'He'll come and try to fight, that's for sure, and that's what people don't understand. It's not about who he is, or what his record is. It's about what he is, and what he stands for, right now. People don't understand that when fighters have something to fight for, it's different.'

Those were interesting, perceptive comments from Wilder, who was being talked up as America's Joshua in that he had the same brutal power in the ring, yet an intelligent, measured approach outside it.

In Britain, the feeling was that Molina could provide an upset but that Anthony and Eddie had chosen him because he should pose no massive threat. There was so much time and money tied up in the negotiations with the Klitschko camp that you could understand that way of thinking. Certainly David Price, the British heavyweight who hoped to take on AJ one day, felt it was a cop-out. He told ESPN, 'They've taken the safer option without a doubt. I always thought that Joshua's team – not Joshua himself – think that Molina is a safer bet. It's less likely that something will go wrong.'

Molina was having none of that, telling reporters at a pre-fight press conference, 'If I can breathe, if I can stand, I'm going to fight to knock him out. Other fighters might say that's what's gonna happen. I'm gonna show you that's what's gonna happen.' Molina had something to prove – which had often been shown to be the best motivation for success in the boxing world. In January, 2012, he was knocked out in the first round by Chris Arreola in front of his hometown fans in Texas. The defeat hit him hard and he temporarily left boxing to become a teacher to disabled children.

The ring bug returned six months later as he beat Andrew Greeley in six rounds in front of the same fans. He had found redemption and went on to win his next four fights before falling to that defeat by Deontay Wilder. Molina explained how his attitude to boxing changed after that defeat by Arreola, saying, 'The world doesn't really know the story I bring to the table. They judge me by one fight, the Arreola fight. You guys could've beaten me. I was weak-minded. But I have grown into a dangerous heavyweight and there is no other heavyweight in the world who has gone through the things I've gone through.'

In the run-up to the Joshua fight, he remained a teacher, explaining to his local paper, the *San Antonio Express-News*, a year earlier, 'I love teaching kids with disabilities because they're underdogs in their lives and I'm an underdog in what I do.' And his view on being the underdog in the Joshua fight could also have been expressed with his other comments to the *Express-News* when he said, 'He's supposed to run over me. That's what he expects. That what everyone expects. But one of the most beautiful things about sports is when that doesn't happen, and the underdog pulls off the upset.'

Eric Molina was clearly a nice guy – the way he looked after special-needs kids back in Texas, the respect he had for other boxers and the decent way he approached boxing, seeing it as an art, rather than pure brutality. Unfortunately, none of that would help him in the ring when he came up against Anthony on 10 December 2016. He would go the way of most of AJ's opponents, knocked out early. But he would have no regrets at coming over to England to take on Anthony – as he told one reporter, 'This [boxing] is not the greatest thing I am going to do in my life.' After the fight he would head back home to Texas and to the classroom, teaching those children who needed him.

He had been knocked to the canvas in the fight in the third round, and the ref had stepped in to call it a night. For Anthony, victory and relief – it could now be announced publicly that he would fight Klitschko. Klitschko stepped into the ring beside Joshua as Eddie Hearn announced the two men would fight each other at Wembley Stadium on 29 April 2017. Eddie said it would be 'the biggest fight in boxing history' and the two men stood face to face, eyeballing each other, but breaking into a smile. It was clear, even at this stage, that each had massive respect for the other. Both Wladimir and Anthony were impressive human beings of intelligence and grace; there would be no hype or trash talk there that night or when the bout finally took place.

From the ring, Anthony said, 'We move on to a bigger arena, more people can view it. This is the step up people have wanted. Klitschko wants his belts back, may the best man win. I focus on myself, that's how I beat Wladimir Klitschko.' While the Ukrainian added, 'He is the best man in the division and the excitement speaks for itself. This is what the fans want and this fight must happen.'

Then Anthony spoke of how he had dispatched Molina, saying, 'It was slow, patient and calculating. You are dealing with someone who is not giving you many options, so I had to create them and, once I saw it, I managed to connect properly and knocked him out. He had maybe two shots, but he is not a Kiltschko; he is not a Haye; he is not all of these other fighters. He was trying to throw a few haymakers, someone who's waiting on the back foot, you just have to be patient and take your chances. I'm consistent, I'm not at my peak yet. I have to keep working. That's why I don't get too hyped, that's why I took him out like I should. I am going to keep on handling business like I should. The belt doesn't represent me, it's how you deal with people, how you represent yourself as a champion. The belt is a sign of a champion but what makes a champion is the things I have just said.'

And Wladimir added, 'AJ did his job. I'm happy he won, that was my wish. There is no other fight to do but this one between us. I was watching, observing, making my notes. I'm really looking forward to this fight. I am a fan of his talent. He can unify the division and be a great champion. My guns are cocked. They've been cocked for a year. Nothing personal, but it's business. My Hall of Fame coach Manny Stewart said, "One day you will have a signature fight." This is the fight he was talking about. It is something outstanding.'

The pundits were also impressed. My friends at the *Sun* pointed out that AJ has the 'fear factor' – 'Joshua is so good he can win fights without even stepping into the ring. Molina – who rocked WBC champ Deontay Wilder last year – was terrified of the Brit and barely threw a punch. The American looked like he would have been happier sat ringside with Joshua's next opponent Wladimir Klitschko watching some other chump get battered.'

Some fans of the fight game felt it had been too much of a mismatch; that Molina should never have been in the same ring. But this was the man who took the great American hope Deontay Wilder to nine rounds not that long before. One fan explained the simmering feeling of discontent, saying, 'Joshua has talent but that was a complete mismatch. The reality is that – as in any sport – there are only a few talented individuals above the average and Joshua is yet to meet one of those. Until he meets someone as good as him it's really hard to say if he is any good. A Klitschko fight will be interesting but is he in his prime?'

And another fan suggested that AJ had only fought 'bums' and that he still had everything to prove, 'If only Joshua was the real deal. But who knows how good he is – he has only fought bums. As a Kiwi I have been wondering whether Joseph Parker's opponents could have been anywhere as lousy as Joshua's recent ring fodder. The answer is no. In fact Joshua, Whyte aside, has been lined up against cannon fodder. Joshua post-Brexit is a great metaphor for Little England. How will we ever know how good he really is? He'll be fighting that ego on a stick, David Haye, next.'

But Eric Molina had no doubt about how good AJ was, and how much potential he had. He had been on the receiving end of a battering in Manchester and admitted he was glad to get out of the city without suffering even more pain. It had been a nightmare time for the man who was so well respected back in America. He made it clear he believed Anthony would beat Klitschko and now go on to reign supreme in the division – and that the only man who might cause him problems would be Deontay Wilder. Eric told reporters after the AJ fight, 'He's a great champion and I personally do not see too many heavyweights beating him, he's very strong. One thing that Joshua has shown is, he's getting bigger, better, faster, stronger, every fight. I don't want to disrespect Klitschko, but the torch is going to be passed that night. If it hasn't been already, I think it's going to officially get passed.

'If he goes through Klitschko, which I believe that he can, there is only one fight left for him after that and that is the fight that everybody knows – the Wilder v Joshua fight. After that fight, I don't really see much else out there for him, maybe Tyson Fury, but yes, definitely he is the present and the future.'

Anthony had done his work – and done it well. He had beaten

Molina, earned the Klitschko fight, enjoyed the announcement in the ring that that bout was on, and was already looking forward to it happening. The fight was four months away and Anthony knew that his preparations would have to be spot on if he were to succeed. But first there would be a much-needed rest period, and a Christmas and New Year to savour. He had certainly earned them.

CHAPTER 13

THE BIG COUNT DOWN

'Anthony could rule the heavyweight division for a long time'
– BARRY MCGUIGAN

It was a fabulous festive season in 2016 for Anthony Joshua. After his victory over Eric Molina two weeks before Christmas, and the confirmation of his super fight with Wladimir Klitschko, he took some well-earned time away from boxing. He spent time with his 'closest and dearest' at Christmas and then had a relaxing break with pals in Dubai come the New Year of 2017. It was ideal for recharging his batteries and taking his mind off the monster fight that would follow at the end of April. The boys then visited Monaco and New York, and then, at the start of February 2017, the holidays ended and Anthony started getting down to business.

He was three months away from the Klitschko bout and he wanted to hit the ring in peak condition on 29 April. He had enjoyed his holidays and was, in 'normal' terms – i.e. yours and mine – still super fit. But that wasn't enough. Anthony Joshua was a perfectionist when it came to his work and only the absolute best would do. He would now work like a demon in the gym, on the road and in sparring to ensure he was in the best condition of his life. He knew the threat Klitschko posed and that any chink in his armour could be deadly. This was world-class boxing and if you weren't right mentally and physically, you were putting yourself in real danger. Because your opponent would be in peak fitness; or at least you had to prepare as if he would be.

Some rivals had looked a tad on the flabby side in AJ's ascent to the boxing summit, but Klitschko would not be in that category. He would be 41 years of age when they fought, but even when he had appeared in the ring after the Molina fight it was clear that he had worked himself into the ground. He had the physique of a man ten years younger – and that would be a boxer in tip-top condition, not one who was fighting to hold back the years.

He also had that motivation we talked about in the Molina chapter. Wladimir had gone to ground after his shock defeat by Tyson Fury in Düsseldorf in November 2015. He hadn't lost in eleven years before Fury beat him on points. He viewed the loss as an off-night but his pride had been badly hurt. He knew that the pundits and the fans were writing him off as a has-been and that he needed to beat Joshua to regain his reputation. It made him a most dangerous opponent. After a period of soul-searching and tough training, Wladimir was ready to return to the ring. He wanted the chance to avenge the loss to Fury and the rematch was set for seven months after the first bout, in July 2016.

But Fury sprained an ankle and then was declared 'medically

unfit' for a second rescheduling for the end of October. The rematch was cancelled and Klitschko was pencilled in for a fight with the promising Lucas Brown. Now Klitschko himself would fall victim to the injury jinx, with a calf injury ruling him out until 2017.

It was now that Eddie Hearn, Anthony's promoter, earned his money by stepping in and suggesting to Wladimir's team that a fight at Wembley in front of 90,000 fans – 'Britain's biggest ever boxing bout' – might be a good, as well as highly lucrative, move for the Ukrainian. It was all agreed – the AJ v Wladimir fight would go ahead at the English national stadium at the end of April 2017, contingent on Anthony beating Eric Molina the previous December.

The Super Fight was on – the fight that would propel Anthony Joshua from being a hero in Britain to worldwide fame.

The immense scale of the fight was first highlighted in the middle of January 2017, when it was announced that 80,000 advance tickets had been snapped up. The second batch of tickets had sold out within an hour when released and the total tickets sold had beaten the record set by Carl Froch's World Super Middleweight title rematch against George Groves in 2014. In a statement, a joyous Eddie Hearn trumpeted, 'The demand for tickets for Joshua vs Klitschko is phenomenal – this is unquestionably the biggest fight in British boxing history and we could have sold out Wembley twice over.

'We have put a request in to Brent Council, the Mayor's office and Transport for London to increase the capacity by a further 5,000 tickets. We are confident of a positive answer and we will release further news shortly. Roll on April 29!'

Eddie could hear the tills ringing and he had also shown his worth by ensuring the TV deals would be premium ones. The fight would be broadcast in Britain on Sky Sports Box Office, under Anthony's deal with Matchroom and the satellite station. And in America, where the really big bucks were to be made, it was reported that HBO and Showtime were battling it out for the US television rights. Showtime had AJ under contract in America, so it looked likely that they would win this particular fight.

But that would not be the case. Ultimately, the two premium cable rivals agreed a deal that would see *both* of their broadcast crews at ringside to produce separate American telecasts. The deal, sewn up between Matchroom Sport and Klitschko Management Group and the two networks, meant that Showtime would televise the bout live and HBO would show it on tape delay.

You could see just what it meant to the networks – and gauge just how far Anthony had come when the boss of Showtime Sports told the world of his scoop. He said, 'We are thrilled to be delivering Joshua vs. Klitschko to the US audience live on Showtime,' Stephen Espinoza said. 'On the afternoon of April 29, US sports fans will be able to tune in to Showtime to join a record-breaking crowd of 90,000 at Wembley Stadium and a worldwide television audience.

'They will witness an event that represents not only the contesting of the heavyweight world championship, but potentially the changing of the guard in the most influential division in boxing. We are proud to be Anthony Joshua's exclusive US television partner as he attempts to establish his legacy against the legendary Wladimir Klitschko, live on Showtime Championship Boxing, as Showtime continues its unrivalled commitment to the sport.'

And HBO Sports boss Peter Nelson was also full of it, even though his network would only be able to show the fight later on. He said, 'Both promoters and both networks have found a solution that enables boxing fans in the US to watch the world heavyweight championship. This agreement ensures that our subscribers have access to same-day prime-time coverage of the fight. It will mark Wladimir Klitschko's 22nd appearance on HBO and the first for Anthony Joshua.'

Eddie Hearn also waded in to tell the world just how big this fight was – and just how much of a draw his boy AJ had become. As part of the prepared statement, he added, 'I'm delighted to announce this historic deal that will see Britain's biggest-ever fight shown on both HBO and Showtime in the US. It takes a special fight to break down barriers and boundaries but also networks and executives who believe in working with the best interest of fight fans in mind.

'With the obstacles in place it would have been an easy resolution to not air the fight in the States, but I want to thank HBO and Showtime for their perseverance and allowing America to see one hell of a fight at our national stadium in front of 90,000 passionate fans. Joshua v Klitschko is a fight for the ages and we look forward to the show!'

Earlier, Klitschko had told fans even he was stunned by the enormous scale of the fight: he had fought in front of thousands of fans in Germany, which had become a second home for him and his brother Vitali for their bouts over the years, but nothing like this. He said, 'Seven times I've fought at stadiums, seven stadium fights, but I've never fought in a stadium with 80,000. I've fought with probably the biggest – 61,000 at Gelsenkirchen where Schalke plays, but 80,000 – that's definitely an upgrade.'

An upgrade it was. It was rapidly turning into one of the biggest fights the world had seen, let alone Britain. The fight had drawn interest across the planet and took me back to the era of Ali and Frazier when heavyweight battles truly were planetary events. The division had flattered to deceive over the last decade or two, with interest on the wane and bouts not earning the interest they had in the 1970s, or the 1980s when Mike Tyson emerged. Now, with the advent of the era of Anthony Joshua and his ability to reach massive audiences with the boxing world *and* outside, that all seemed set to change. The age of the blockbuster in heavyweight boxing was back with this fight. In lighter divisions, such as middleweight, Floyd Mayweather had proved a winner as he drew in the crowds but the heavyweights had not been of similar attraction – until now. The big characters and personalities had been missing, boxing had become predictable and a tad boring as the Klitschko brothers dominated.

But now this fight, in April 2017, was building up day by day, week by week into something akin to a rock concert by the biggest band in the world. Everybody wanted a piece of the pie. Neither of the biggest cable TV networks in the States wanted to be left out and neither did the fans. It was fast becoming a legendary event that would no doubt be spoken about for years to come . . . but it was a boxing match, not a music concert, or even football's World Cup final.

In the modern era I cannot think of another boxing match

that had drawn such massive interest in Britain *and* America. This was the crux of Anthony Joshua's appeal and the clever way he and his management team were plotting his future. Both HBO and Showtime had wanted to show the fight because they had heard and seen for themselves how AJ was powering through the heavyweight division. They had been told he could be a modern-day version of the late, great Muhammad Ali – he did, after all, have the looks, the personality and the fists to follow in his footsteps if every piece of the jigsaw eventually fell into place. Although even Anthony would laugh off such a suggestion; Ali will always be *the* Greatest in his eyes and any comparisons he viewed as ridiculous. But the fact remained that he had become the most in-demand boxer in the world – after just 18 professional fights. Beat Klitschko and that demand could only intensify.

The extra tickets would be agreed and would sell out, meaning a crowd of 90,000 would be at Wembley to cheer Anthony on as he battled for the title.

By February, Anthony was well into his training schedule and shared a picture with his fans of him on a bike in the gym up at Sheffield with heart monitors and a facemask to check his oxygen and fitness levels. He stuck to his usual pre-fight training regime, which meant heading up to Sheffield to use the Team GB facilities at the centre of excellence during the week, then heading back home to London for the weekends. At the start of March, Anthony shared another pic with his fans on Twitter, showing him with his trainer Rob McCracken in Sheffield. He captioned it, 'Shattered! Analysis then home for the weekend baby.'

The assessments of the work he had put in, plus the chats with Rob about how things had gone, and whether they were bang on target, or some aspect needed extra attention, were a key part of the week up in Sheffield. As per other fights, AJ stayed over in accommodation for the athletes who trained there. It was simple and stark but ideal for what he was doing. Luxury was out, but the basic rooms kept him hungry and determined to stay on course. His food was packed and provided each day, so that there was no worries about what he was eating or whether he was getting the right nutrients. The meals were prepared in advance and all he had to do was unpack them and eat them.

Then it was time to meet up with Rob and work through another punishing shift. Anthony met him each day without complaint, although he was 'knackered' at the end of it. He knew that over in Kiev and, closer to the fight, the Austrian Alps, Klitschko would be being put through schedules that were just as testing and demanding. There was no room for any complacency if he were to overcome the challenge of the Ukrainian master. Wladimir would be going to any lengths to be seen as the rightful champion again.

The training schedule worked out by McCracken had AJ on his knees at times, such was the intensity. The idea was to build up gradually after he returned to training in February and build up to a peak in March and the start of April and then to revert to a less punishing routine as the fight loomed. That way Anthony would not be exhausted when the bout itself began. There was no point in working to perfection and then finding your man had nothing left to give in the ring itself. McCracken was quite brilliant in his approach. He had the old-school sensibility that you worked damned hard but also the modern-day intelligence to use hi-tech fitness equipment and analytical machines to hit the perfect level.

Both men were helped, of course, by the fact that they had the use of the Team GB boxing facility at Sheffield. Not that it was a one-sided 'gift': Anthony was always happy to spar with would-be Olympians during his training and offer help and advice to the boxers. And Rob, in turn, was happy to lend an ear if the lads wanted an opinion on their training or work in the ring. It was the perfect arrangement as AJ loved preparing for his fights there and the Team GB lads enjoyed having a champion in their midst.

In many ways, McCracken had become to British boxing what Dave Brailsford had become to British cycling, before he was caught up in controversy after all his success: a leader who took the sport into advanced territory. Brailsford employed traditional methods such as physical fitness and tactics but was also eager to embrace technological developments. The Welshman was famed for his monitoring key statistics and tailoring training sessions to improve any areas that had been shown to not be 100 per cent on target.

Before the 2008 Beijing Olympics BBC Sport summed up the brilliance of Brailsford's approach, saying, 'He has been hailed as the genius powering British cycling's resurgence as a world force and as his MBE proves, such a view has royal assent. The former competitive cyclist in France has progressed through the ranks into British Cycling's top job. The sports science academic, also an MBA business graduate, has combined his sporting knowledge and business acumen to create a much-revered

Olympic programme that could transform Team GB to a squad that has the potential to return from Beijing draped in gold.'

In much the same way, Rob McCracken revolutionised the British boxing approach and it was a magnificent coup when Anthony persuaded him to become his professional trainer. Rob would continue his role with Team GB, so both AJ and British boxing benefited. As Brailsford had been a promising cyclist himself, so McCracken had done well as a boxer.

The tough sessions continued into April for Anthony before winding down a week before the fight with Wladimir. AJ had given his fans a glimpse of his training on his Instagram and Twitter accounts. 'It looked exhausting just to look at them!' one fan told me. 'It's unbelievable the amount of training a boxer goes through for months before a fight. During the days of Ali and Foreman it seemed as though training only stepped up a gear in the month before a bout, but now it's much more intense and methodical with all the analysis and tests that go on.'

In the rundown to his previous fight with Molina, Anthony had given fans a glimpse of the more unusual methods he employed. Probably more old school than McCracken would suggest, it focused on him lifting weights with his teeth to strengthen his neck muscles! The Instagram snap showed him with a towel in his mouth and two kettlebells tied to the towel, which he then lifted up and down! He captioned the move 'Old school tekkers' which probably sums up the move – it hardly fitted into McCracken's hi-tech, advanced vision of training.

One fan took a light-hearted view of the teeth routine – commenting that it 'looks like an exercise that Suarez would fancy!' That being, of course, a reference to the former

THE BIG COUNT DOWN

Liverpool striker Luis Suarez who had sunk his teeth into Chelsea's Branislav Ivanovic in a Premier League clash in 2013. The Uruguayan had also been suspended for similar incidents while playing for Ajax in Holland in 2010 and for his country against Italy in the 2014 World Cup in Brazil.

Other fans did not take the Instagram pic as lightly, with some using it as a vehicle to question whether it highlighted AJ could be in danger for the fight with Wladimir. Whether it highlighted him as being too addicted to seeking a bodybuilder's frame, a sort of modern-day Frank Bruno, who perhaps went for a sculpted physique at the expense of heightened mobility and technique. One boxing aficionado summed up the fears, questioning if Anthony was 'a proper, real heavyweight boxer', 'I like Joshua and he is probably the best boxer we have had for a while. But there are still questions that need to be answered. Has he got a good chin because he has only been hit with one good punch, off Dillian Whyte, and it rattled him. He had to take cover and recover. Can he last for the full 12 rounds against someone who he can't knock out for the full 12? One thing I know for sure, if he was around in the 1980s and 1990s he would have got slapped silly by some of them boxers – Lennox Lewis and Mike Tyson – these men where proper real, heavyweight boxers.'

Another fan elaborated upon that theme, adding, 'No doubt about it, Joshua has a big physical body, more suited to be a bodybuilder rather than a boxer. Can he last 12 rounds? Has he ever gone 12 rounds? Can he take a punch? And the answer is we just don't know. We don't know because he's never fought anyone half decent who's got a punch. He keeps fighting opponents who couldn't fight their way out of a paper bag. And until he does, you can't say he's any good.'

The Instagram pic of the towel weight-lift had clearly stirred up emotions and doubts. Even then, my opinion was that, yes, Anthony did have the physique of a bodybuilder, sculpted and lean, but he ALSO had the mobility and technique. No way was he lumbered by his physique as was Frank Bruno. Big Frank often found it hard to escape from danger because he was musclebound but AJ had already proved he could 'float like a butterfly' to quote the great Ali. He had power and mobility, like the Greatest, and that made for a sensational, dangerous boxing talent.

Ironically enough, in the current heavyweight division, only Wladimir came close to that ability: he was a big, sculpted man but was light on his feet and could move in for the kill *and* duck danger with surprisingly nimble feet for such a giant. A boxing fan from London confirmed my belief that Anthony did have the skills necessary to fight with, and beat, the best because of his physique, rather than despite it, 'All heavyweights have a punch, decent or not. The trick is not to get punched. He has been but stood up to it. The opponents he is fighting are top ranked heavyweights in the IBF, which is exactly what he's supposed to be doing. He is the IBF champ.'

In August 2014, Anthony had joined Wladimir at his training camp in Austria. He went to spar with the then champion and was even given some guidance by the Ukrainian's own trainer, Johnathon Banks. The first contact between the two men who would clash at Wembley in the 2017 megafight came in the build-up to AJ's Manchester bout with Konstantin Airich and

Wladimir's with Kubrat Pulev in Hamburg, Germany. After the sparring, Anthony would tell reporters how he enjoyed the sessions and how he respected the man he would one day beat. He said, 'I felt I belonged there but Wladimir is different to everyone else. He's been the champ for 10 years; he's in a league of his own. For me to be where Wladimir Klitschko is, there's a lot of work to be done. I can see myself potentially being there but to own it and make it look easy, there's a little bit of work to be done. I feel I am talented enough to become the world champion but to stay there for as long as he has, keep defending the titles and stay hungry for it, that's what I need to learn.'

Anthony would add that the sessions were invaluable in that they helped him 'learn to defend'. Such was the intelligence of Klitschko that he was willing to help his young sparring partner improve in an area that he had mentioned as being one he was particularly keen to work on. The two men helped each other over in Austria: AJ helped Wladimir prepare for his imminent championship fight with his own ring skills, particularly his nimble footwork and heavy punches, and Wlad turned tutor in advising his eager young 'guest' how to improve his defences.

It was typical Anthony, respectful, humble and always willing to learn. It showed how much he liked Klitschko as a person and how he appreciated his talent as a boxing legend. In turn, Banks told RingTV.com at the time of how he, as a rival trainer, liked Anthony and sensed his enormous potential, 'The funny thing is that I was just training Anthony Joshua in camp with Wladimir. I was giving him hand work and all of that stuff. I think that he's a really good fighter, man, and he can fight. I like him. I like him a lot.'

Kevin Johnson and Dillian Whyte, both of whom had felt the power of AJ at professional level, had been among four boxers brought in to spar with Wladimir back then. At the time, Wladimir showed his mutual respect for AJ by tweeting, 'Anthony Joshua is in camp for sparring. Two Super Heavyweight Olympic gold medallists in one ring – that's unique.' I do not seem to remember him tweeting about Whyte or Johnson's arrival, which just goes to show how the Ukrainian saw Anthony as being of different potential even in 2014, three years before they would meet in the ring at Wembley. They would spar for 20 rounds in Austria and Wladimir would admit that AJ did stand out from the other sparring partners. His comment that he 'could feel his athleticism' supports my earlier theory in this chapter that Anthony was far from being a modern-day musclebound Frank Bruno. Klitschko could see even back then that the boy was mobile despite his physique – that he moved around the ring easily, and could both escape danger and pose danger because of that flexibility, when they sparred.

A few days before the Wembley showdown in 2017, Anthony went into a little more detail about those sparring rounds three years previously. He told reporters in more detail how Wladimir had helped him and how the trip had been immensely worthwhile in seeing how a champion set up a training camp. It opened his eyes to how he himself should operate as his career, hopefully, progressed towards a similar level. If it worked for Klitschko all these years of domination, it was not to be sniffed at – once again, AJ showed he was open to learning from the best – how to ally what he would term 'wisdom' with 'hunger'.

He told the press conference, 'I'm not a gym fighter, so I didn't go to prove anything in the sparring. I went there mainly to see how the champion sets up training camp. But our sparring was good. Wladimir kept it technical. He would try and manoeuvre you with his jab and put you in position to throw his right hand. He's patient and he was just trying to set me up, so he could throw his shots. And I was working on defence, jabbing to the body, jabbing to the head. And then I'd go back to the corner, and one of his trainers would say, "Stick it on the champ." And I would say, "Nah, nah. I'm not here for that. I'm not here to prove anything. I wanna watch. I wanna analyse." And that's what I got from sparring, just how he operates in the ring and I learned how a champion sets up training camp.'

Klitschko would go on to tell HBO Sports, 'I believe we learned from each other well. We spent 20 rounds of sparring with each other in the camp, and we know what to expect. So we're well-prepared. He knows that. I know that as well.'

Anthony's preparations also included eating the right foods at the right time. During training he would consume around 5,000 calories a day which included wholegrain carbohydrates such as brown rice, wholemeal pasta and wholemeal bread. On fight day itself that would become white rice and white pasta, and white meats. He revealed that his final meal before entering the ring would be taken around four hours earlier. Caffeine was cut to a minimum during fight week but allowed on fight night with the thinking that it would provide an injection of energy.

At the Beats by Dre launch for the 'Be Heard' campaign, Anthony outlined in more detail the efforts that had gone into his training for the previous fight against Molina – efforts that would likely be replicated for the Klitschko bout. He spent 98 days in the training camp and had 392 organic meals. There were 28 physio sessions and he consumed 210 protein drinks and 420 litres of water. The food detail was meticulous and primed him in perfect condition for that fight. It highlighted the importance of having a nutritionist as part of his team and the way boxing had changed so dramatically over the years. No longer was it enough just to turn up after steak and chips and a glass of milk and expect to win! Nowadays the fight game had progressed dramatically and the smallest details had become key to the biggest wins.

Anthony also outlined his training schedule, which involved 220 miles of interval training, 660 rounds of sparring and 210 miles of running. Again, there was no random figure – it was all detailed to the minute level. He would do exactly that, not a round more of sparring nor a mile more of running. And those exact measures of work would leave him in absolute peak fitness, and ready for battle with his opponent. There was also a revelation that left some commentators baffled – but once again it showed how boxing had developed over the decades. Anthony said he took 98 fish oil supplements in camp and had 950 acupuncture needles in his body in the three-month camp. He confirmed, 'It was 98 days in camp — 392 organic meals, 28 physio sessions, 210 protein shakes, 42 strength sessions and 98 fish oils. I had acupuncture – that is 950 needles in my body. There were 660 rounds of sparring and 210 miles of running. I weigh 249lb. That's the biggest and strongest I've been. And I will do it until my body cannot physically do it.'

As the Klitschko fight loomed ever closer AJ's personal nutritionist Mark Ellison revealed he was unusual for a heavyweight in his food and training. Mark told the online gambling firm firm, Betway, that 'Josh is a freak'. He added, 'There's no other heavyweights like him – that are as lean as him, as athletic as him, that can cope with the training he does. He's the only heavyweight I know that trains like a middleweight.'

Mark said he was involved in the planning and scheduling of meals and that science plays an important role in that he analyses blood biochemistry and body composition. He added, 'He is an unbelievable athlete. He's unbelievably committed, he focuses on the details and he works his absolute nuts off. The challenge for me is making sure he eats enough. We ease a lot in with liquids. These are extra calories that we have to hide in his diet so that it is palatable.'

Betway revealed that a typical AJ breakfast would include: a bowl of porridge, a bowl of fruit, two slices wholemeal toast, five poached eggs and two cups of Greek yogurt. Lunch would be two salmon fillets, two jacket potatoes and a salad. And dinner would be a whole chicken, a plate of hummus, a cup of white rice, half an avocado and mixed veg.

As for Klitschko, his own training camp in the Austrian Alps had pushed him to the brink. The week before the fight, he was looking healthy and supremely fit. A Sky TV team had watched him train in Kiev before he moved on to Austria as part of their agreement to show the fight exclusively in the UK. They had noted how he would stop during sparring and closely observe Anthony boxing on a background screen near the ring, which seemed to play his fights over and over. They said he 'paid attention to every detail', knowing he would have to develop his boxing and mobility to cope with the much younger man. He was said to like 'being the challenger' and was 'bubbling' at the prospect of taking on the younger man who was seen as the 'next big star' of the heavyweight division.

In April, the Sky team moved on to see how Klitschko was doing in Austria. The channel's boxing expert Johnny Nelson said he believed the camp, on the German border in the east of Austria, was perfect for Wladimir. The way Johnny described it – basic, freezing and back to nature – brought to mind Rocky's training camp on a ramshackle farm in Siberia, miles from nowhere with no luxuries. Freezing water and logs for weights, a primitive environment to sharpen him up! Wladimir sounded as if he had taken a note out of Rocky's book as Johnny said, 'For Klitschko, I think this sets him up mentally, if you have to get up in the freezing cold every morning, having to motivate yourself mentally as well as physically.'

By the end of April 2017, both AJ and Wlad looked ready for battle. Anthony was fit and happy with how things had gone. Sure, training was tough and living the life of a hermit was tough. But he was mega confident all the sacrifices would be worth it come 29 April. And hundreds of thousands of Brits would be praying he was right, and willing him on to glory. His build-up couldn't have been better, he had done everything right, his team had done their bit and now it was time to walk the walk. Yes, AJ's moment of truth – and his opportunity to become a legend of British sport – had finally arrived.

CHAPTER 14

I AM LEGEND

And so to that 'Apollo Creed' moment, with Anthony making his entrance to the ring like the American boxer in *Rocky IV*. The fanfare, the visuals and the neon provided a colourful backdrop as the more reticent Klitschko waited his arrival in the ring itself. But would it prove to be merely a showbiz distraction – and a sign of AJ's possible over-confidence – when Big Wlad hit him like Drago had pounded Creed? Or would Anthony take it all in his stride – he was, after all, famed for these extravagant entrances by now – and batter the Ukrainian? Could he separate the showbiz side from the harsh reality of spit, sweat and, yes, blood that the bout itself could harbour?

The answer would be a firm 'yes' – of course, he could. He believed in the extravagance as a reward to his fans; a sign to them that he was confident and that he wanted to put on a show for them. Both inside and outside the ring. Not just now, but for every fight he would take place in. It was part of the deal. The fans paid a lot of money to watch him and they deserved to be fully entertained. Never once did it occur to him that the razmattaz would reflect negatively on him, or his state of mind. He enjoyed it as a final bit of fun and a chance to salute his loyal fans. And then, when he entered the ring he put the showbiz out of his mind and focused 100 per cent on the job in hand.

Doling out pain and defeat to whoever stood across from him in the opposite corner.

Which, in this case, meant the legend Wladimir Klitschko. The man whom he respected, admired and from whom he had learned much about being a human being and the art of top-class ringcraft. Theirs was a relationship that far outweighed the trash talk and antics Tyson Fury had brought to the table when he fought Wladimir; or the similar base level Dillian Whyte had resorted to before AJ destroyed him.

But the mutual respect would be put aside; left well outside the ring as Anthony and Wlad did battle. There could only be one winner, and any sentimentality could prove fatal with both men so perfectly primed for the world's biggest fight of the year. Both had summed up their feelings, hopes and a sort of personal statement of intent in a press conference in New York's Madison Square Garden, where some of the most legendary bouts of all-time had taken place, prior to stepping into the Wembley ring. Anthony told reporters, 'I'm a man who likes to perform. The obsession has always been there for me and not just in boxing. It starts with self; boxing is a representation of who I am. I'm determined to become the best. That's my obsession. I'm a man who likes to perform and entertain and that's always been there. I've always wanted to take on the best.'

Those comments encapsulated Anthony's belief that you could entertain *and* perform. They justified his snazzy ring entrance because he also understood you had to fully back that up within the ring.

He then added, 'God would never put me in a position I couldn't handle, fighting Wladimir Klitschko in front of 90,000 people. But the objective still remains the same.'

Wladimir then outlined his belief in that press conference and a later one at his training camp in Austria that the fight would answer a lot of questions that had been posed about his own position in the boxing world – as well as Anthony's. He told reporters of his respect for his young rival and how he knew he 'was different' from other fighters he had sparred with or watched. He believed AJ would benefit from meeting him in the ring, whether he won or lost,

'I'm fighting a man that I was, is and will be a fan of since I watched Anthony Joshua win his Olympic gold medal in 2012. He was my sparring partner in 2014 when I trained for Kubrat Pulev. He got a chance to look and be in the background of my training team, my camp and got to know a lot. I got to know him in the ring. He was one of many sparring partners. Some of them I don't remember. But I do remember Anthony. He impressed me with his attitude. He was very raw. He carried himself well. He was very athletic and he could box. I was there in the arena in London when he won Olympic gold. Every medallist in the heavyweight and super-heavyweight divisions at the Olympics has to be considered successful. Look back in history.

'He has a lot of potential and so far he has done good. Look, 18 fights, he's a champion and he is fighting the biggest stage in his career. Even in my career I haven't fought in a 90,000 stadium. He started young and he's had success. I've had Olympic champions in my camp and former world champions. I liked AJ's attitude. He was not trying to impress anybody. He backed off, was sitting on the side, not talking too much. He was watching, learning, asking questions. He was very polite. He was different than others at this stage of experience and achievements in sport. You can't see everything. There's so much involved in it. But he got pretty much where I train, how I train, the rules. He got the vibe.

'I believe he has a lot of skills, he may well be the biggest star in boxing. I know there are plans to fight [Deontay] Wilder after me. It's good to be young and ambitious, but I believe this fight has a lot of questions. Is it too early for him, too late for me? All those questions will be answered on April 29, do I still have it, or is it too late? I'm looking forward to his challenge, I have my goal to become three-time world champion and I'm obsessed with it.'

That was honesty for you – and helped explain just why AJ looked up to the Ukrainian and had such respect and time for him. Wladimir had even suggested he would 'help' Anthony to become a champion, if the Englishman lost to him at Wembley. Rarely have such civility and respect been displayed outside the ring before a major fight. It was a joy to behold after the trash talk of previous bouts and how some of the combatants had seemed determined to drag the sport into the gutter.

Even AJ's promoter, Eddie Hearn, appeared caught up in the decency of the pre-fight talk, putting aside the financial considerations that had made the event possible. He made clear his views clear to reporters, saying, 'It's a pleasure to be involved the biggest boxing event in British boxing history. It would be so easy for Anthony Joshua to continue selling out the biggest arenas in the UK while fighting less than world-class competition. It would be so easy for him to do what every other fighter has done and keep knocking out the easy targets.

'But that is not what Anthony Joshua is all about. In his 19th fight, Anthony is stepping up to fight a true legend in Wladimir Klitschko – and isn't that what boxing's all about? What sport is all about? Creating nights and moments that people will never forget – 90,000 people in the biggest stadium in the UK.'

And the magnitude and ever-increasing excitement of the bout had a string of ex-heavyweight boxers and current ones, including champions, making public predictions on the likely outcome. Former champ George Foreman said, 'If I were a gambler, I'd see Joshua as a 5–6 favourite – so I'd put him just in front. But Klitschko knows how to win and how to use his body size. It will be a difficult fight for both of them. If Klitschko wins again…oh my God, can you imagine?' George went for Anthony to win.

Audley Harrison also went for AJ, saying, 'For Klitschko to win, Joshua will either have to run out of steam or make a big mistake at a crucial period. This is Joshua's first step up to a new, uncharted level. Wladimir's experience makes him favourite yet I believe Joshua can upset the apple-cart.'

But Tyson Fury had doubts about AJ, and predicted Wladimir to triumph, 'Klitschko to KO Joshua. Just my opinion.'

And current American golden boy and WBA champion

Deontay Wilder also plumped for the Ukrainian, saying, 'My heart is for Joshua but my mind is Klitschko. I don't think Joshua has the training or experience. When you're fighting a certain calibre of fighters and then you move all the way up to the guy who was the ruler of the division, it is a big leap.'

Boxing great Carl Froch also went for the Ukrainian, saying, 'Klitschko is an ageing fighter but with age comes wisdom and experience. Wlad was unbeaten in ten years until he faced Tyson Fury and that was an awkward, torrid night for him. We may just see the best – and last – of Klitschko.'

The great Evander Holyfield also went with Wlad, saying, 'Joshua is one of the heavyweights who is a complete fighter. He can box and had a great amateur career. Klitschko should be able to out-manoeuvre him with his skill of mind. But if Joshua doesn't give him a chance to do that, what's going to happen?'

And even Brit legend Lennox Lewis had his doubts, even though he was one of Joshua's biggest admirers and flag wavers. He said, 'Anthony has knocked out everybody, so what has he learned? Where is the experience? Wladimir is almost on 70 fights so you've the experience, the old against the new and the strong. Can Wladimir's body take any more? I'll take experience but only slightly.'

The fight was the talk of the boxing world and beyond as the celebs and fans took their seats at Wembley that warm April night. Excitement and expectation was rife as the two boxers came out of their corners on the first bell. The bout effectively boiled down to three key stages – in the fifth round, when Anthony knocked Klitschko to the canvas, the sixth round when Wladimir somehow recovered and floored Anthony with a huge right and the eleventh round, when AJ again had the Ukrainian on the canvas twice before forcing the ref to intervene as he battered him relentlessly in a corner of the ring, ending it with a massive right uppercut.

One boxing fan wrote on Twitter that it was the moment 'Klitschko's soul left his body'.

Klitschko had not been stopped for 13 years – the last time came in 2003 when he was KO'd by Lamon Brewster.

Of course, that it is simplifying this magnificent encounter and stripping it back to its extremes. In between those pivotal moments, the fight swayed in one fighter's way, then the other's. AJ had got off to a belter, attacking and looking as if he wanted a quick knockout, culminating in that fifth-round hammer blow that had Klitschko down but not quite out. Then Wlad had hit back, from looking weary and old to almost delivering that sixth-round KO. Then Anthony seemed to take a breather – and a big gamble – as he tried to recompose himself and find fresh strength. Wlad could have KO'd him as he tried to draw breath. AJ then re-emerged strongly and battered Wlad, leading to the eleventh-round denouement.

Two of the three judges had Anthony ahead on points at the time of the eleventh-round KO, the other saw Wladimir as the winner. American judge Don Trella had Aj ahead 96–93, while Puerto Rico's Nelson Vazquez scored the fight slightly closer at 95–93. The third judge, American Steve Weisfeld felt that Klitschko had put in the better display of the two men, having him in front at 95–93 heading into the eleventh. The idea that AJ could have *lost* but for that KO had some punters who were not fans of his jumping on a bandwagon that suggested he was a little bit lucky, and that he should have beaten a 41-year-old more comprehensively.

One boxing fan said, 'Joshua was very fortunate to have won that fight. If Klitschko had steamed on into him after knocking him down, the fight was over there and then. In the 6th round. Halfway through – and where would Joshua be now? A potential has-been rather than being talked of as the greatest boxer in the world. Joshua is limited to that big punch, has no real ring skills and is tactically naïve. Just wait till he is put in with someone like [Deontay] Wilder. He will expose his flaws and knock him out, no problems.' Another fan said, 'AJ got lucky, very lucky.' While another added, 'Amazing win for Joshua. But surely this fight does more to prove how great a fighter Klitschko is/was. Would Joshua have beaten Klitschko if they were both in their prime? Doesn't look like it. Obviously life doesn't work like that but Joshua v Fury will be one hell of a fight.'

But others dismissed those views emphatically, pointing out that Wlad had shown he was far from finished, and that AJ's performance was actually quite brilliant. He had done what had been asked of him and the knockdown in the sixth, far from being disastrous, could eventually be viewed as a key moment in Anthony's career. He would now not want to repeat the experience – but at least he had experienced it early in his professional career, and dealt with it. As one fan siding with Anthony proclaimed, 'AJ wins by knockout, after a torrid 6th round that could have easily been curtains for him. He was hit with some great shots from VK; he weathers the storm and comes back to knock the guy out in the 11th, and still some people are knocking him. For crying out loud he won, and won well, and he will destroy that idiot Fury.' And another member of the Joshua boxing fan club, claimed that the Brit would have beaten Wladimir in the peak of his career, let alone when he was aged 41, 'Klitschko in his prime would have to concede some of the wisdom, experience and ring craft that he has now. He'd be relying on youthful strength and power. Both of which Joshua has more of than Klitschko ever had in the first place. He would have lost worse. Just as he did against Lamon Brewster. Think about it…since Brewster he has fought no one good. David Haye being probably the biggest scalp in that time.'

Yet another AJ fan praised the boy as being 'the real deal' and believed he could unify the heavyweight division by beating all contenders and pretenders, 'Joshua is the real deal. Sure he was being outboxed for some of the fight – but when he got knocked down he got up and finally finished the job. He is smart enough to recognise and learn from his mistakes and his boxing skills will develop. But what can't be learned is the character that he showed in getting back up, maintaining his composure and desire and finding a way to win like a true champion. The only person close to him at the moment is Tyson Fury, I'd love to see Fury get fit again and take out the wildly overrated Deontay Wilder and then for Josh to do Joseph Parker to set up a massive reunification bout!'

What was apparent and stood out at the O2 was the immense bravery of both Joshua and Klitschko; the tactical brilliance of both men and the power of both men. It made for the most thrilling, and best, heavyweight fight since the Holyfield/Tyson bouts and, arguably, surpassed them, bringing to mind the legendary Ali/Frazier fights of the 1970s. It was old v young and that in itself posed a brilliant backdrop to proceedings. The stagecraft and craftiness of Klitschko versus the exuberance and energy of his young rival. This was a fight in which Anthony Joshua had to grow up quick – and he did just that. By the end of proceedings both men had put on a master show of boxing. Both deserved all the garlands and acclaim that had come their way.

And it was pointed out that there had been an iconic moment in the eleventh round after Anthony had delivered that stunning right uppercut. He stood over Klitschko as the veteran lay flattened on the canvas, with his right glove still extended above the prostate Wladimir. The scene was captured by the press photographers for posterity and, when it made the next day's papers it could have been a mirror image of another great British fighter, Henry Cooper, when he flattened Muhammad Ali, then known as Cassius Clay, in their fight in 1963. As with Joshua and Klitschko, the fight was at Wembley. And, just as it was AJ's 19th pro fight, so it was Ali's 19th too. Cooper stood over the flattened Ali just as AJ had with Wladimir, both with right hand extended as if ready to punch in case their victim got up. But there the similarities ended. Ali had been floored in the fourth round in June 1963, but recovered to win in the next round. Then, in his next fight he beat Sonny Liston to win the world title. This mirror image pic was talked about in the press as one of the many reasons why Brit boxing fans were hoping that Joshua might become 'the British Ali'. Of course, that is possible, given their respective good looks, boxing power and personalities out of the ring, but Anthony still had a hell of a long way to go to achieving such legendary status, despite his wonderful victory over Klitschko.

Anthony showed he was a boxer with both intelligence and respect for other fighters when he spoke in the ring after his victory. He said, 'What can I say, first and foremost, 19 and 0, three-and-a-half years in the game. I'm not perfect but I'm trying. I want to give a shout out to all my trainers, to 90,000 people in the arena, and lastly, as boxing states, you leave your ego at the door and you respect your opponent. So a massive shout to Wladimir Klitschko. In terms of the boxing hall of fame he is a role model in and out of the ring. I have nothing but respect for anyone who steps in the ring. I'm a little bit emotional, I dig deep. If you don't take part you will never know. London, Germany, Ukraine, I love you.'

On being knocked down he added, 'This is boxing, I'm only going to improve. When you are in the trenches that's when you find out who you really are. There are no complications in boxing, anyone can do this, just go in and keep on digging. You can see, I won, that's how I had to dig. I fought my heart out. And Fury, where you at baby? I enjoy fighting. Tyson Fury, I know he's been talking a lot, and he wants to compete. I love boxing, I will fight anyone now.'

Klitschko then spoke to the crowd, telling them they had been awesome and thanking them for their generosity to him. They had applauded him and never booed him – he was, after all, a great former champion and a man who had contributed massively to a great night for boxing and, indeed, the image of boxing as an honourable sport. He had given everything and deserved all the accolades that would now come his way, both on the night and in the days that followed. It wasn't every night you got to see a *real* legend of boxing perform in England. And for all the complaints that the era of Wladimir and his brother Vitali had made the heavyweight game stale, the brothers had proved they were giants as they beat fighter after fighter.

Wladimir told the O2 crowd, 'I hope you enjoyed the fight, the best man won tonight, it's an amazing event for boxing. Two gentlemen fought each other. I say gentlemen because boxing came from England. It's really sad that I didn't make it tonight. It didn't work. All respect to Anthony, though, congratulations.'

This had certainly been a different Klitschko to the one who had struggled against Tyson Fury. Looking back at that fight, you can't help but consider the theory that, most unusually, Wlad had taken his eye off the ball. He may have thought Fury was merely a brawler and that he didn't need to be at his sharpest, or his most tactically astute. Certainly, he appeared well short of energy and ideas that night. He looked lacklustre and struggled to get going – all of which added to the theory that he had indeed been a tad complacent in his training and attitude towards the fight, although he and his management team denied that was the case. Which they would, of course, because that would be a dereliction of duty, a cheating of those fans who had turned out and spent big bucks to watch him fight. They put the result down to an off night; a freak outcome and one that would not happen 99 times out of 100.

There was no feeling in the Joshua camp, or even among his fans, that this fight was simply the crowning of the new young king against a has-been golden oldie. All involved on the Joshua side expected Klitschko to be reinvigorated and rock hard to beat after his Tyson Fury loss. If they needed any reminding, Wlad's trainer, Johnathon Banks, reminded the press of other so-called 'over-the-hill' ex-champs who had come back and proved they still had it. And that if Anthony was thinking it would be a walk in the park, he would be sorely mistaken. Banks told reporters, 'That would be like when Michael Moorer thought when he fought [and lost to the ageing] George Foreman. And what George Foreman thought when he fought [and lost to] Muhammad Ali in Zaire. George took what Ali did to him and did the exact same thing to Michael Moorer. There's something about when an old man don't back down from a fight, you better pay attention to the older guy. There's something he knows that the young guy don't know.'

But, of course, AJ never for one moment believed he was in for an easy night – and lucky too! I believe Klitschko would have beaten Tyson Fury if he had fought him that April 2017 night at the O2; he was magnificent, even in defeat.

The breakdown of the fight shows that Anthony had the 90,000 crowd on their feet in that eleventh round when he finally put Klitshcko to bed for the night. The win meant he had retained his IBF title and added both the WBA and IBO titles to it. His left eye looked a little puffed out but it was nothing compared with the damage he had done to Wladimir's left eye, which had cut and bled throughout the bout.

But Anthony would later admit he knew if he could mentally and physically overcome the setback of being knocked down in the fifth round, he could win. In the sixth, he even had the audacity to tell Wladimir that he would beat him if Wlad did not knock him out in the round! Speaking of the moment he spoke to Klitschko mid-fight, AJ told broadcaster Colin Murray at Finchley ABC, that he warned Wlad, 'If you let me get through this round, I'm gonna *beep* [f***] you up.' Wlad then told him, 'I'm going to knock you out.'

AJ added, 'I knew these two rounds were vital, I knew it was close. I stepped it up, boom, boom, boom, boom. Subconsciously, I don't know where it came from, I just whipped it up and saw his chin . . . it was like an exorcism where he's looking at the back of the crowd. He started trying to disguise when you're hurt and I thought this is my chance to take him out and I just tried to land every punch, I threw the kitchen sink at him and I finally got him out of there in the end.'

If that makes you think that AJ had resorted to trash talk after all the 'gentlemanly' behaviour he and Wlad had exuded before and after the bout, think again. It was just throwaway jibes in the ring that even the most civilised fighter gets involved in during what is essentially a war. One man against one man and immense pain if you get it wrong on the night: a coliseum where even a few mind games, and choice words, can help in a battle that is mental and spiritual as well as physical, if the rivals are fairly evenly balanced gladiators. Wladimir would also bad-mouth AJ during the fight, telling him that he would 'knock you out, motherf***er'. So each man had a dirty dig at the other; it did not alter the respect they have for each other or the way they conducted themselves before and after the fight with much-lauded civility and genuine mutual admiration.

Britain's David Haye, a boxer who loves to indulge in trash talk and did so in a big way before his fight with Tony Bellew the previous month, had warned AJ that being as nice and civilised as he was could hit him in the pocket. That it did not sell seats or encourage pay-per-view TV firms to battle over your rights. He told the *Sun*, 'I have never had any beef with Joshua whatsoever. He's not a Bellew type, he wants to be friends with everybody. It's quite endearing. But in terms of being a popular heavyweight champ who generates pay-per-view sales you can't want to be your opponent's best friend every time.'

That argument was hardly a strong one – hadn't Joshua's fight with Wladimir sold out at Wembley, with 90,000 fans wanting to see the fight? And the TV pay-per-view figures were astounding. All this, with both men insisting on being civilised both before and after the event. But at least Haye predicted AJ would win, adding, 'Who wins? Joshua, definitely. He's the guy on the up.'

There was no shortage of praise for AJ after the bout. Fellow boxers, sporting stars and celebs made their views clear, many on Twitter. Boxer Carl Frampton tweeted, 'You can't question Anthony Joshua heart and balls now! What a fight.' Football's Match of the Day host Gary Lineker said, 'So gripping was the fight that the 3 of us in the studio jumped up when Anthony Joshua won. At least it was during a match edit.' And London mayor Sadiq Khan tweeted, 'World heavyweight champion. Londoner and legend – congrats on a stunning victory in front of 90k home crowd.' While former Oasis singer Liam Gallagher tweeted, 'The only sport that truly deserves the big bucks.'

Former Man Utd and England defender Rio Ferdinand said, 'Anthony Joshua dug deep & showed it's great having talent but when all said & done grit & determination in the trenches is what gets you through real testing times. Salute the champ! Klitschko showed real class in defeat too . . . something I wish I could of [*sic*] had a bit more of if I'm really honest!' The ex Chelsea and German international Michael Ballack tweeted, 'Great fight, great run, great spirit #JoshuaKlitschko #Obsessed.' While Real Madrid superstar Gareth Bale was keen to pay respects to both parties, writing on Instagram, 'What a fight! Congratulations Anthony Joshua and huge respect to Klitschko.' Former footballer turned Sky TV pundit Jamie Carragher was appreciative of the efforts of AJ and Klitschko, writing, 'What a fighter & warrior Klitschko is at 41, but what an experience to come through for Joshua!'

And 'Iron' Mike Tyson, former heavyweight champion, added his own tribute, telling ESPN, 'This one fight has changed boxing. It's going to be all about Joshua and the heavyweights now. The sky's the limit for Joshua. He's going to dominate the division and make so much money if he keeps doing what he did at Wembley. Joshua is still a baby but now he's the biggest name in boxing and people only pay big money to see the best.' Tyson's tribute led some fans to analyse if Anthony was on the same level as the man who initially blasted all opposition put in front of him. One boxing fan summed up the general feeling, 'I don't think AJ is as good as Tyson at his best . . . yet. And that's a big point – he's still learning. Klitschko was a brave choice. Keep learning in a fight like that. The easy choice would have been to pick a chump. It says a lot about AJ but what's important now is he doesn't let it go to his head and learns from it – and doesn't forget he was probably one good combination away from losing.'

Eddie Hearn had boasted that the fight was the biggest ever in Britain, and that had proved to be absolutely the case, in terms of the crowd at Wembley and the pay-per-view TV figures. It also made dramatic inroads into the American market, which was important if Anthony was to achieve that much-heralded aim of becoming the sport's first billionaire boxer.

The TV viewing figures released after the fight showed just how big a star AJ was about to become if he continued demolishing his rivals. Obviously, the figures also reflected Wladimir's world standing – but the fact that Anthony had downed him suggested he was on the brink of worldwide mega stardom. The figures highlighted how the bout had been one of the most watched ever – taking the sport back to the glory days when Ali would pull in massive audiences.

Hearn said it had smashed the 1.5-million figure set by Manny Pacquiao's defeat to Floyd Mayweather on Sky Box Office. Hearn told Radio 5 Live, 'We broke British Box Office records on pay-per-view.' And in America, the fight averaged 659,000 viewers on Showtime where it was aired live. Figures peaked at 687,000 viewers during rounds five and six – a big increase on Anthony's previous Showtime numbers. The delayed tape-replay on HBO was watched by an average 738,000 viewers and peaked at 890,000. It was only the third time in history that the two big US rival channels had bought into a heavyweight title clash.

Over on German TV channel RTL the bout was watched by an average 10.43 million viewers. The whole card in Germany, including the other fights on the bill, averaged 9.59 million viewers. This beat the 8.91 million that tuned in to watch Tyson Fury take on Wladimir in 2015. Even in Poland, the average viewership was an impressive 920,000.

In total, the fight aired in almost 150 countries.

Wladimir's manager Bernd Bonte had told the *Daily Telegraph* that it had produced massive international interest – bigger than any his fighter had known over the years of his and his brother Vitali's domination. He said, 'In the David Haye fight we had close to 16 million viewers on German television. It's generated a lot of interest in Germany. This is one of the few heavyweight fights in the last decade that creates a worldwide interest. The international sales are bigger than ever, for any fight the Klitschkos have done.'

Of course, Anthony was delighted with the outcome, both in terms of boxing progression and the boost to his bank balance! He had previously told *GQ* magazine, 'When I first started my career the aim was to become a multi-millionaire. But now there are ordinary people worth millions because of property prices. So I need to be a billionaire. Being a millionaire is good – but you have to set your sights higher. If I'm making £10 million from my next fight, my next target has to be making ten times that.'

Given his success and profile, it was hardly surprising that Anthony had already signed sponsorship deals with Jaguar, Lucozade, Lynx, Sky Sports, StubHub, Texo Construction and Under Armour. And his promoter Eddie Hearn reckoned there was lots more to come: after the victory over Klitschko AJ's profile had risen considerably, so there would be even greater demand for a piece of him. Companies weren't stupid: they knew a good thing when they saw it, and were always keen to invest in a sportsman who would boost their own profile and image. With Anthony Joshua, they would receive a tonic in both those areas, given he was now the unbeaten world heavyweight champion in three belts and was as popular, and likeable, in Britain as Frank Bruno had once been.

And Eddie Hearn was convinced it was down to Anthony that the fight had been in such massive demand – and that the demand to watch him would only increase as he got more and more successful. He said, 'You can't be in a key market and not see an Anthony Joshua billboard. Someone sent me one today from Dubai. Another one was sent to me in Los Angeles and in Germany. He's everywhere. And we're only scratching the surface.

'Anthony wants to keep going for 10 years, and if so, that journey will evolve through fighting in different markets. It's the only way you can do it. He probably can't go back to arena fights in the UK because it's like any job — how can you earn what you're going to earn on Saturday and then take another fight for a third of that amount? So I think the challenge will be to break down barriers and new markets, whether it's Africa, the Far East, Middle East, America.'

The world was certainly in Anthony's hands, but I have a strong feeling he would also like to have fights in the UK in front of his fans. I understand Eddie wanting to push him to an ever-wider audience, and fights in other countries, but I believe AJ feels a real loyalty to his UK fanbase and would like to continue fighting on home ground. Sure, widen his audience and financial reach, increase his sphere of dominance worldwide – but never forget the British fans who put him up there in the first place.

CHAPTER 15

JOY DIVISION

After beating Klitschko, Anthony took a few weeks away from the fight game. Deservedly so, the training, build-up and bout itself, plus the aftermath interviews with the press, had left the Watford lad exhausted. Not that he would initially admit that: indeed, straight after the fight he had claimed he could do it all over again straight away! Luckily, his excellent advisers and backroom team talked sense into him, advising him to go relax on a beach and do nothing but have fun, laughs and some good food with his pals. Enough was enough, now it was time to indulge himself a little. And he did just that.

In the aftermath of his brilliant victory, there was a period of reflection in the UK papers as they tried to pinpoint where exactly AJ stood now, in terms of boxing and as a man who was becoming a major celebrity outside the ring. It was telling during the fight that there were many women in the crowd at Wembley and that he was popular across gender and generations, with young, middle-aged and old all taking to him.

You just had to look at his Twitter feed to see how many young women were tweeting to him about how they had got tickets to the Wembley showdown with Wladimir – and how much they were looking forward to it to see how broad Anthony's appeal had reached. Sure, some pundits would argue that it was down to his good looks, but it also had much to do with his personality and friendly character. And who is to say that women can't enjoy a night out at the boxing to savour the sport itself? It would be gross misogyny to suggest that they bought their tickets purely to ogle a man. Look at the crime-book market – women are the biggest buyers of the genre. You would think men would be given to the bloody outcomes and savagery! Same with the controlled violence of the ring, surely? Yet women are rapidly buying into the sport with the advent of Anthony and the likes of Nicola Adams in women's boxing. Nicola indeed has the same fabulous personality as AJ out of the ring and the same brutal skills within it, and Nicola's popularity and success in the Olympics and now as professional fighter – again like Anthony – also helps explain the rise of female spectators at the biggest matches.

After the win, he was as likely to pop up on a TV or radio chat show, or in a spread in a magazine or paper's feature section, as much as on the back pages. He had tremendous crossover appeal – and, consequently, marketability, because of his engaging personality. As my good friend Dave Kidd, top columnist at the *Sun*, pointed out that Anthony was, 'as brutal as a young Mike Tyson in the ring. And as likeable as Frank Bruno outside it.'

Dave added, 'It's a combination as powerful as anything that Anthony Joshua unleashed on Wladimir Klitschko on Saturday night. A combination that will surely make him the biggest and wealthiest star in British sporting history. Joshua had been a heavyweight champion of the world for 12 months. On Saturday, he became *the* heavyweight champion of the world — the rightful heir to Muhammad Ali, Rocky Marciano, Joe Louis and Iron Mike. For generations, their crown was the single greatest sporting title on the planet. And the thrilling manner of Joshua's victory – in front of 90,000 punters and a record pay-per-view TV audience in excess of 1.5 million restored lustre to the grand old crown . . . the salt-of-the-earth charm. The deep booming chuckle. The national treasure with the crown jewels to match. There is nothing affected about Joshua's intoxicating normality . . . He will now have greater commercial value than any modern British sporting greats like Andy Murray, Gareth Bale, Lewis Hamilton or Rory McIlroy – although he insists that he should not be compared to them until he has been at the top for longer.'

The comparison with Lewis Hamilton is a particularly valid one. I compiled the first biography on the Formula One star back in 2007/08 and pointed out back then that he had the crossover appeal to make millions outside the racing arena as well as within it. He was liked by women and men because of his engaging back story and personality. And that proved to be a good prediction because Lewis, like Anthony, ended up dominating his chosen sport *and* often being at celebrity bashes for music and the general entertainment business. He made millions outside of F1 with his various sponsorship deals and endorsements.

Also like AJ, he shook up a sport that had become rather dull and unmarketable. Lewis arrived to blow away the cobwebs of the Michael Schumacher years of domination, just as Anthony did with the Klitschko brothers' era of power in boxing. Not that Schuey or the brothers Klitschko are to be denigrated for their ability to win and keep winning. No one was good enough to break up their domination on a permanent basis and in boxing and F1 that only adds to their brilliance in staying at the top for so long. It was just that the two sports had become relatively boring and predictable. It was only with the arrival of Lewis Hamilton and Sebastien Vettel in F1, and Anthony Joshua in boxing that new ground was made.

That opened up the sports and made them more popular as more people took an interest in them. The new heroes – Lewis and Anthony – were also charismatic and relatable to, again unlike Schuey and the Klitschkos, and that broadened their appeal and brought thousands more fans flocking to see them in action. Lewis and AJ didn't save F1 and boxing, as no way were they dying, but they did breathe new life into them. Fresh excitement and thrills and spills in sports that had lacked them as the giants of former eras continued to dominate. And the money men behind boxing and F1 were certainly grateful to Hamilton and Joshua for bringing the disciplines to wider audiences. It meant more readies from gate receipts and TV coverage which, in turn, meant the protagonists could earn more and the biggest showdowns would become major events once more.

Former champion Mike Tyson spoke out to warn AJ to be careful with the millions he was about to make. 'Iron' Mike had earned a fortune and blown it in a rapid mental decline after becoming world champion. He agreed that the rise of Joshua had revitalised a sagging heavyweight division and said he saw a lot of himself in Anthony in the ring, in how he demolished Klitschko after being floored in the fifth round by him, 'Joshua showed heart. He went down from a big punch by Klitschko but he didn't give up, he got back up. That was real intestinal fortitude. There's no quit in him. I also love that he goes out to hurt his opponent. That's what boxing is all about but most fighters don't have that hunger.'

Speaking at the opening of his Boxing Academy in Dubai Tyson also said he understood why some pundits had outlined similarities in his upbringing and Anthony's, 'Sure I see the comparisons. If you are of an Afro-English background you're likely to have a tough time. If you're born in the wrong part of town it's always going to be rough. You're going to be financially challenged, scholastically challenged. It was like that for me and it's like that now. Boxing gives kids like me and Joshua an outlet. You can take a guy with nothing, clean him up and the next thing he's meeting the President of the United States or the Prime Minister.'

A clear indicator of Anthony's growing popularity came when he was installed as the favourite to win the BBC Sports Personality of the Year award days after his defeat of Klitschko. The fans, the press and the general public were all clearly enamoured with how Anthony had treated Wladimir with respect, as well as with his engaging personality. His trainer Rob McCracken said of this approach, speaking to the *Daily Telegraph*, 'He's a really nice person, Anthony. He's very level-headed. Same as he was six years ago. Not changed a bit. Charismatic, people like him, and he's great for British boxing.

He's identical to how Carl Froch was. He'll fight anyone. The opponent isn't an issue. The work ethic is second to none, his discipline. He lives the life. Different, styles, but very similar to Carl in the discipline, the hunger, what they want to achieve. They're willing to do whatever it takes to get there.'

A sign of Anthony's worth to firms' images came when Lynx made him one of their 'Men of the Moment'. Their explanation of the category also helped highlight Anthony's status outside the ring. Lynx said the mission was this, 'Young guys live in a world filled with labels and limits. In fact, over 50% of them have been told that a real man should behave a certain way. Pressure that ultimately makes bullying, depression and suicide so common among men. #isitokforguys kicks off Lynx's mission to expose the pressure guys feel to "be a man" and empower them to be whoever they damn well want. Together with our partners, we want to fight those limitations and create a society where there is no wrong way to be a man. No labels. No limits on what men can or cannot be.'

This was truly something worthwhile for Anthony to be involved with. To help young men challenge stereotypes and understand that it is OK to say you are not OK. Lynx had chosen him because he had the following decent attributes: tolerance, open-mindedness, talent and class. The full tribute read like this, 'The British public have always had a soft spot for talented heavyweight boxers. In Anthony Joshua they finally have one with huge amounts of both talent and class. Anthony should also be lauded for showing solidarity with Muslims, despite the huge amount of online abuse he knew he'd receive. Open-mindedness and tolerance are British values we must never abandon.'

Anthony was chosen for the 'Men of the Moment' campaign by Lynx along with the likes of Prince Harry and Dele Alli, the Tottenham and England footballer. Also included were the actor Luke Evans, the musician Jonas Blue, the singer Craig David and the actor Dev Patel. They were a group of young men who were well respected and who wanted to make some sort of difference to the world they lived in. It was a worthy cause and reflected well on them all.

Anthony had told the *Guardian*'s Kevin Mitchell how he was keen to help others less fortunate, 'I like to give, for sure, to help people. That's important. I want to invest because I like business. I know for a fact there is some kid somewhere who has watched what I'm doing and is, like "I can do that". He'll find himself in a gym and, somehow, he'll go on and do better than what I've done . . . The issue people have with politicians is, how can you talk about what's happening in certain areas when you haven't lived in certain areas? I can definitely relate to a lot of people. I wouldn't mind doing prison visits, giving people a bit of inspiration, and just helping.'

Anthony's boxing hero was a man who also wanted to leave his imprint on the world outside the boxing ring. Muhammad Ali, 'The Greatest', was someone many people looked up to and many idolised for his boxing, charitable work and oratory. And many pundits and fans were labelling AJ 'Britain's Greatest' after his demolition of Klitschko. The *Sun* called him the 'heir to Ali's throne'. Anthony admired and respected Ali and his achievements and would love to be a British version of the great man, although he laughs off such an idea when asked. However, on his official website Anthony eulogises

Ali's life and achievements, saying, 'The King of the Ring, the man who brought finesse to the game, the larger than life character... Cassius Clay, who became Muhammad Ali. The most intelligent of fighters who illustrated that although brute force is important, smarts can always outdo the force. Whether it's his long list of titles or his equally dramatic personal life, the one thing that shines through it all is his integrity and his humour. Still today his fight against George Foreman that became known as 'The Rumble in the Jungle' is still considered one of the greatest sporting events of the 20th century.'

Once again, it is instructive to note the words AJ employs – words similar to those that had been applied to him for that Lynx campaign to help young men. 'Intelligent', 'integrity', 'smart', 'finesse' and 'character'. These are the traits that are important to Anthony along with the acceptance that you need to be fast and brutal in the boxing ring. The two would not seem natural bed partners, but they are what set AJ, Klitshcko, and in his time Ali, apart from the run-of-the-mill brawlers who tend to inhabit the ring and not contemplate achieving a charitable or powerful legacy of aid outside it.

Two of Anthony's other idols emphasise the demands he places upon himself within the ring, the steel and big heart Evander Holyfield possessed in abundance, and the tactical genius of Lennox Lewis. Of Evander, AJ says, 'Evander "Real Deal" Holyfield was crowned Heavyweight Champion of the world in 1990 after defeating James "Buster" Douglas and once again in 1993 after coming out on top in a rematch with Riddick Bowe. I loved watching his fights where he tucked up on the inside and would constantly work and slip. He did everything his trainer would ask for really. A man with a massive heart.'

And his view of Lennox Lewis goes like this, 'Lennox Lewis won gold at the 1988 Olympics before turning professional. He's the last undisputed Heavyweight Champion that we've had since Bob Fitzsimmons in 1899. If I manage to repeat his success, that will mean Britain will have had an undisputed Heavyweight Champion in the 19th, 20th and 21st centuries. He showed us "The Sweet Science of Boxing" and a simplicity to winning masterclass fights. Lewis retired after successfully defending his title against Mike Tyson. He remains one of only three fighters to end his career with no unavenged defeats.'

So what now for Anthony Joshua? There was talk of a rematch with Klitschko. That would make good financial sense but did it take Anthony any further down the road in his boxing career? It could well happen, but I believe he would be better off taking on Tyson Fury in a 'Battle for English Pride'. Fury had beaten Klitschko and boasted that he would beat Anthony with one hand tied behind his back. It would be a blockbuster of a fight and victory would set AJ up for a bout that could well prove the defining one of his career. Against the powerful American Deontay Wilder, who is fearsome and brutal in the ring. Wilder could be AJ's Frazier to his Ali. He would test Anthony to the limit and it would be a fight the whole world would want to see.

Anthony would most likely have to fight him in Vegas, but he could hold out for the bout to take place in Madison Square Garden in New York. Boxing's most iconic mega venue and the arena where AJ's biggest heroes, including Ali and Lennox Lewis, had enjoyed legendary battles. Yes, that would do it – Fury first at Wembley Stadium, then Wilder in New York. Win both those two fights in two awesome venues and his name would be written in legend.

By the summer of 2017, Anthony Joshua had already made massive strides towards that legendary status. He had won three world titles, made contributions to society outside the ring, was pulling in millions of pounds in prize money and endorsements and was being called 'the modern-day heir to the Greatest'. He had come a mighty long way in just 19 professional fights – but was the sort of guy who would force himself to go a mighty long way further. That was in his natural make-up: a young man who wanted to never stand still, to always be moving, always be advancing in the boxing world and in his life. He was a young man who liked to have a plan and defined goals for his future, for the day when he eventually would hang up his gloves. He had ambitions outside the ring, motivated by his intelligence and that inherent need to be an achiever, whether that be in business or charitable efforts.

This is a good man, a man who has revived the sagging spirit of heavyweight boxing and who has turned his own life around from petty crime to career success, being universally liked, admired and respected. A truly triumphant tale of personal redemption. Yes, Anthony Joshua is a winner – and is determined that no one will get in his way as he marches ever onwards to world domination. A British heir to Muhammad Ali. Go now, AJ, go . . . float like a butterfly, sting like a bee.